Carried West

Carried West

One Family's Journey Through Famine, War, and the
American Frontier

By Parker Corbett

Unbound Press

Carried West, By Parker Corbett

Copyright 2026, Unbound Press

All images remain the property of their original copyright owners. All images used are properly credited whenever possible. If any rights holder believes an image has been misused, please contact jandajtk@outlook.com to arrange proper credit or remove the image. If images are not credited, they were created by the author. All efforts have been made to ensure originality and avoid infringement.

The publisher and author do not warrant or represent that the contents within are accurate and disclaim all warranties and are not liable for any damages whatsoever. Although all attempts were made to verify information, they do not assume responsibility for errors or omissions. All content is provided 'as is.' This edition reflects information available as of [March 2026.] References to real organizations, products, devices, or services are for identification only and do not imply endorsement or affiliation. Where research findings or statistics are cited, sources are provided in notes or references. Absence of a citation does not imply universal consensus.

ISBN Paperback ISBN: 978-1-971207-31-5

ISBN Hardcover 978-1-971207-32-2

The American Inheritance Series: How national events shape ordinary lives.

This series tells the story of the United States not through presidents, generals, or famous turning points alone, but through the lived experience of one family moving across generations. Wars, migrations, economic upheavals, technological change, and social transformation are not treated as distant historical forces. They are shown as pressures that reshape daily routines, alter opportunities, fracture communities, and redefine what survival and belonging mean.

From immigrant streets and frontier farms to battlefields, modest towns, growing cities, and modern suburbs, each volume follows ordinary people navigating extraordinary moments. National events arrive not as abstractions, but as disruptions — to work, to family structure, to identity, and to the future imagined for the next generation.

Grounded in documentary research and narrative reconstruction, the series reveals how history is experienced from the inside: through uncertainty, adaptation, loss, resilience, and reinvention. Together, the volumes form a generational portrait of a nation in motion, showing how the forces that define eras ultimately take root in kitchens, fields, factories, schools, and homes.

Table of Contents

Dedication

For Chase and Hudson.

Go West, young man, and grow up with the country.

— Horace Greeley

FAMILY ORIGINS

JANE MARGARET CHAMBERLAIN

1916 — Los Angeles, California / 1990 — Oceanside, California

Daughter of

LAWRENCE SAFFORD CHAMBERLAIN   1873 —

Topeka, Kansas / 1965 — Coronado, California

and

MABEL LUCILE POWER

1890 — Kansas City, Kansas / 1978 — California

Third Generation

Benjamin McMeekin   and   Jennie Marie Safford

James Power and Margaret Gertrude Stealy

Fourth Generation

Hayden D. McMeekin and Mary Jane Lawrence

Jacob Safford   and Esther Coon

Walter Daniel Powers   and   Maria Ramsden

William "Billy" Stealy and Catherine Quinn

Preface

Carried West

I did not go looking for Billy Stealey. He appeared the way the past often does—unremarkably, in a column of faded ink. Born in New York around 1842. Orphaned young. Sent west. Drummer boy in the Civil War, and dead before middle age.

The trail that led me to him started in 1970, when my father developed what he called "the genealogy bug." Armed with a tape recorder, he interviewed his grandmother, Mabel Lucille Chamberlain, who spoke of forgotten tales, family lore, and hardships and pioneer lives. She was eighty then, her memory reaching back to a world of kerosene lamps and dirt roads, to stories her mother had told her about coming west as a child. Decades later, when I found that recording, it became a doorway—not just to Billy, but to the forces that carried him, and eventually my own parents, to a California coast in 1968.

My parents met in Laguna Beach that year. My father was a California native, born and raised in Los Angeles and Beverly Hills. His high school classmate was Nancy Sinatra, and her father, Frank, sang at their graduation. Their house on Beverwil in Beverly Hills bore the ZIP code that would later become shorthand for celebrity and wealth: 90210. From the outside, it appeared to be a life cushioned by privilege and advantages.   Behind the lush lawns and stucco homes lay a childhood marked by fracture—divorce, isolation, and the restless movement between grandparents' homes that defined his early years in the 1940s. Nations carry mysteries, and so does family history, and appearances rarely tell the whole truth.

For my family, the pattern wasn't new: their lives had been shaped by motion and by the necessity of being pushed somewhere else.

My mother had come from the Midwest, trading the biting Chicago wind for palm trees and salt air. How my parents arrived at that moment is a story that stretches far beyond them. It reaches back into an America that had not yet become America—into territories that would later be called states, into wagon roads and rail lines, into cities still assembling themselves out of dust and ambition. It crosses California, Kansas, Missouri, and New York; over the Atlantic back to Ireland, where famine forced relocations, and then to the American frontier when the Orphan Trains again altered the course of families' lives for generations.

Neither knew they were following paths worn smooth by the people before them— tracks that began not in choice, but in necessity. Famine. War. Displacement. The restless American belief that life could begin again somewhere farther west.

I grew up hearing fragments of these journeys: names without context, places without maps, and family legends that flickered at dinner conversations or when my dad had too many glasses of wine. There was talk of an Irish archer and an English lady, though no one could say quite when or where they had lived. There was the Topeka "Judge," who "built the railroad," and the scandal of the ancestor who served on the Bleeding Kansas bogus legislature, whose name was rarely spoken above a whisper. There was a sea captain, maybe a pirate, we were never sure, who came home from an extended voyage and picked peas on Sunday, for which he was arrested. The story and that particular scandal had survived for 400 years. These tales continued not because they were complete, but because they were repeated often.

My father's research filled boxes with census records, ship manifests, military rosters—data points that suggested direction but never quite resolved into a story. When I inherited the collection, the stories became mine to try to understand. And in them, I found William.

The archive created more questions than answers. In the 1860 census, he was listed as a thirteen-year-old boy living in the household of John and Eliza Mackey in Monmouth, Illinois—far from New York, far from any family that shared his name. The notation was sparse: "William Stealey, age 13, born New York." No parents listed. No explanation for how an Irish immigrant child ended up on an Illinois farm.

I traced him forward through time. In 1862, he enlisted as a drummer boy in the Illinois Infantry. He was fourteen years old, though the recruiter recorded him as eighteen—a common fiction for boys eager to serve. He survived Shiloh, Corinth, and the Siege of Vicksburg, mustered out in 1865, returned to Illinois, where he married, raised children, and died in 1884, not yet forty-two.

But the question that haunted me was simpler than any of that: How did he get to Illinois in the first place?

The answer, when I found it, was a single line in the records of the Children's Aid Society of New York. He was listed on what would later be called an orphan train—one of thousands of children sent west to relieve the overcrowded tenements of New York and provide labor for expanding rural farms. The society's ledgers recorded his departure but not his arrival, his placement but not his story.

That absence became the shape of this book.

As I followed William's trail, I discovered something unexpected. The lines I was tracing—Stealey, McMeekin, Safford—did not run parallel. They intersected. And when they did, they revealed a deeper pattern: these were families carried to opposite sides of America's most violent divide. Some fought for the Union. Others settled in Bleeding Kansas, where the question of slavery turned neighbors into enemies. By the time my great-great-grandparents married in the 1890s, they were uniting lines that had once stood on different sides of the nation's fault line.

This book traces that movement across a century of upheaval. What begins as survival becomes something more complicated: a story of division, loyalty, and the forces that shape identity when history leaves no choice. This is not a story about choosing sides. It is a story about what happens when history leaves no neutral ground. Some families observe history. Others are carried by it. This is the story of how my family crossed famine, war, and the frontier—and what it cost to arrive.

Introduction

I am two years old. I don't remember this afternoon, but I will return to it decades later.

We have made the hour-long drive south from our modest rented house in Corona del Mar to visit my grandmother, Jane, and great-grandmother, Mabel, in Coronado. The family has gathered at the house on "C" Avenue, a home that is both residence and an arrangement of status.

My father is comfortable here. After his parents' divorce, when he was ten, this was where he spent countless nights and weekends while the adults around him tried to reassemble the remnants of their fractured lives. Their marriage had been tumultuous, full of instability, alcohol, and strain. In later years, he would describe Mabel as one of the only steadying influences of his childhood—a source of order, warmth, and predictability when much else felt unclear.

Here, in this house, the world briefly made sense. The rooms are cool and shaded, despite the California light pressing insistently at the brocade curtains. The air smells of pine furniture polish and freshly cut gardenias from her yard.

My father is recording the conversation.

He is sitting on a dining chair pulled too close to the coffee table, a tape recorder balanced carefully on his knee. The reels are turning with a soft mechanical insistence, catching every word, every pause, every correction before it can disappear. He is twenty-nine years old and a new father. He does not fully grasp what he is trying to preserve, only that something is slipping. My voice can be heard on the thin, wavering tape: a young baby squealing with delight upon seeing the cat next door. Across from my dad sits Mabel, who has lived in this home for nearly 60 years.

Mabel tells stories of her own father, James Power. He arrived, she recalls, from Newark, England, as a stowaway on a banana boat. He was eighteen years old and had nothing. She laughs as she tells my father, probably not for the first time, the improbable detail that he ate so many bananas during the crossing that he could never bear the sight of them again. My dad thinks it sounds like more family folklore — one more story to note with curiosity alongside the others. Years later, I will confirm that this one is entirely true.

Today, Mabel is dressed, as always, for an occasion no one else arrived for. She is eighty years old and composed as though she is about to receive visitors from another continent. Her dress is printed with deep, embroidered flowers — burgundy, gold, and forest green — gathered neatly at the waist and falling in disciplined folds to below her knees. A strand of pearls rests at her neckline, not ostentatious but declarative. Her white hair is arranged in soft waves reflecting effort and habit. Even seated, she carries herself with the upright confidence of someone who has never quite relinquished the idea that lineage can be worn like a garment.

Her living room reflects the same sensibility. Heavy lamps with pleated shades cast beams of amber light. Upholstered chairs sit in precise conversational groupings, as if awaiting guests who have only stepped out momentarily. Antique tables hold framed photographs whose silver edges have dulled to a respectable gray. Everywhere there are objects that imply continuity: cut-glass bowls, embroidered runners, porcelain figurines with expressions of permanent discretion. The house does not display wealth so much as a particular kind of breeding.

In the background, my grandmother Jane — Mabel's daughter and my father's mother — moves in and out of the conversation like a current beneath the surface of a river. She holds a glass in one hand, the ice cubes of her Tom Collins clinking softly with each gesture. She interrupts frequently, correcting dates, adding color, challenging certain myths, even as she helps sustain others. There is affection in this, as well as competition. Memory, in this house, is not neutral territory.

Mabel, however, is unhurried.

She speaks of people who exist only in outline — an English sea captain who once picked peas on a Sunday and thereby committed a minor but memorable scandal against propriety. An Irish archer, though no one any longer remembers what wars or hunts might have occurred, and the "Lady" he married, evoking yet another family mystery. My father presses: Who was the English captain? Where did the Irishman come from? What was his name?

Mabel answers, but not in ways that resolve anything. The stories arrive in portions, and the details dissolve under scrutiny. What is offered is not history, but proof of inheritance — stories repeated often enough to survive, even when they are no longer understood.

My father tried to capture what he could. Notes were taken. Dates compared. Questions framed with increasing urgency as the realization grew that a generation capable of bridging nineteenth-century experience and the contemporary one would soon be gone. History had become personal, and it suddenly felt finite. Twenty years from now, I'll discover these notes and recordings and assemble the stories that they've preserved.

That afternoon in Coronado would not have mattered if it had ended there. For most families, it would have. Stories would have remained stories — repeated at holidays, disintegrating over time, stripped of context but preserved for their emotional toll. Names would have continued to drift, slightly altered with each retelling. The past would have stayed indistinct.

But my father did not leave it alone. In the months that followed, the tape recorder became a tool. Interviews expanded, and his research accumulated. He wrote letters requesting information from relatives, societies, and archives. What had begun as curiosity hardened into a refusal to accept that the story would remain incomplete.

But the further he looked, the thinner the evidence became. Dates conflicted, names shifted in spelling, or vanished entirely. Stories repeated for years with complete confidence could not be substantiated, while others dismissed as exaggeration started to reveal unexpected elements of truth. In 1970, this was no simple undertaking. Before the internet, before ancestry websites and digitized print and searchable archives, tackling genealogical research meant writing physical letters, visiting courthouses, spending hours on reels of microfilm, and enduring extensive waits for replies that often never came. With a full-time job, a wife, and a new baby, he made progress, but eventually resigned himself to historical silence.

After being given my father's research in 1990, I began my own attempt to assemble the scattered pieces into a story that made sense. From that afternoon in Coronado, the story reaches backward through states and oceans—through Kansas and Missouri, through New York tenements and orphan trains, through famine-scarred Irish villages and English industrial towns.

Instead of going out with friends to the clubs and popular raves of my day, I often stayed home with papers and hand-drawn charts spread over the dining room table, trying to make sense of who had told me what, where one line crossed another, and which mysteries still refused to yield. I wondered about the "Irish archer from Kentucky." Was he a soldier? Why Kentucky? Had we really come from Southern ancestors who stood, as my mother put it, on "the wrong side of history"? At first, I was drawn most strongly to the outcasts, the losses, and the hard edges of the story.

The search was a personal endeavor. The less we understand what our forebears feared, wanted, or defended, the less we understand ourselves.

As I moved from generation to generation, I noticed a common pattern in my family's story: a series of displacements. Ireland to New York. New York to the interior. Children removed, reassigned, sent west. Lives interrupted by war. Families reassembled in unfamiliar places.

What does it mean for a family to be carried?

Not to move by choice alone, but to be pushed, redirected, reorganized by events that arrive without invitation. Famine. Urbanization. Industrialization. Each generation encountering a different version of the same problem: how to survive the moment they have been given, and how to position the next generation to do the same.

The story, if it could be called that, did not move forward in a straight line. It shifted under pressure — economic, social, political — responding to forces far larger than any single decision.

An Irish archer.

An English lady.

A drummer boy.

A judge.

They were anecdotes that suggested a continuity, but never fully explained it. Until it arrives in a room in Coronado, where it is spoken aloud and preserved on a two-dollar cassette tape.

When the conversation ended that afternoon in 1970, the past had spoken — not always clearly or completely — but it had given the next generation enough clues to eventually find the truth. Millions of Americans descend from individuals whose lives were imperfectly documented or not at all; however, their decisions influenced future generations in profound ways. Relocation, adaptation, and reinvention remain central themes in our country's ongoing development. Understanding them demands attention not only to what can be proven, but also to what must be inferred.

Silence, too, becomes part of the record. It reminds us that history is always incomplete, that for every recovered story there is a larger field of forgotten experiences. Acknowledging this limitation does not diminish the value of research. Instead it situates the search within a tradition of inquiry that values humility as much as discovery.

Part 1— From Famine to Frontier (1840s)

The Legacy Begins

—————————————•◆ ◆•—————————————

April 6, 1862 — Shiloh, Tennessee
William "Billy" Stealy, age 16

DAWN HAD NOT YET broken when he woke. The damp, cool air along the Tennessee River had settled into their wool blankets and clothes throughout the night. Around him, men were still sleeping—some on the ground, some wrapped in coats, others half-awake in the way soldiers learned after weeks in the field. Camps stretched through the trees, quiet except for the occasional cough, the low murmur of a voice, or the shift of movement.

He did not carry a rifle. He carried time. The drum hung where he had left it, the strap worn soft from use, and the shell dulled by weather and handling. He lifted it into place by habit, settling the weight against his body. The sticks felt familiar in his hands. This part required no thought.

An officer nearby gave the order—quietly at first, routine, like every other morning—and Billy stepped forward a few paces into the open space between tents. He raised the sticks.

Reveille.

The first notes broke the stillness cleanly, sharply, carrying through the trees. A pattern every man knew before he was fully awake. It did not ask. It told.

The camp stirred immediately. Blankets were thrown back, and men pushed themselves upright, some swearing under their breath, more already reaching for boots and belts. The rhythm continued, steady and insistent, cutting through the fog of sleep. It was structure imposed on reluctance, on exhaustion, and on the simple human desire to lie still a few minutes longer.

Billy did not look at them as they rose. He watched the officers. Another signal came—subtle, a gesture, a word—and he shifted instantly into the next call.

Assembly.

The tempo changed. Faster now. Purposeful. Men moved more quickly, pulling on coats, forming into companies, tightening lines that only moments before had been scattered shapes in the half-light. Muskets were lifted. Cartridge boxes checked. The camp was becoming a machine preparing to move. The regiment stretched through the trees, thousands of shapes in blue wool. Billy's drum would tell them when to advance or retreat when gun smoke made voices useless.

There was a tension under it now. Officers speaking more sharply. Men glancing toward the tree line, toward sounds not yet fully understood. A distant crack—maybe a branch, maybe something else. Then another.

Billy heard it, but his hands did not stop. The drum had its own sequence, its own authority. He followed it as he had been taught, as he had practiced in camps and along country roads through Missouri and Kentucky. Rhythm first. Always rhythm. Then the order came—clearer now, more urgent.

To arms.

The change in the pattern was immediate. Harder strokes. Faster. The sound traveled farther now, no longer just waking

men but pulling them into readiness. Lines tightened. Voices
rose. The shape of the regiment snapped into place.

More cracks echoed through the trees. Not branches.
Gunfire. Billy did not need to be told what it meant. He had
heard enough in the months before to know the difference.
Even so, he watched the officers, waiting for the signal that
mattered. It came quickly: forward.

Billy struck a driving cadence, a rhythm meant to move
bodies, to push men ahead even when instinct told them to
hesitate. The sound cut through the growing noise—shouted
commands, the clatter of equipment, the first real volleys
rolling in from the edge of the camp. Men stepped past him
now, forming ranks, moving toward the trees where the firing
had begun.

Billy stayed where he always did, just behind the line. Close
enough to see them disappear into the smoke beginning to
gather between the trees and to hear the shift from scattered
shots to sustained fire. Close enough to feel the ground change
underfoot. The camp was becoming a battlefield.

He kept playing. The sun was just beginning to rise when
the line was fully engaged. And somewhere in that rising light,
the morning—ordinary just minutes before—was gone.

❖

November, 1854 —Bleeding Kansas
Ben McMeekin, age 6

THEY CAME IN BEFORE dawn. Wagons rolled in from
Missouri, wheels grinding over the same roads used for trade,
but today they brought no goods. Groups of men rode in
armed, organized, and purposeful. They were not settlers and

had no intention of staying. They had come for a single act—to cast a vote where they did not live—to ensure the outcome of the election was not in doubt. Thousands of pro-slavery men crossed into Kansas that day. They were called Border Ruffians, sometimes called "Southern Yankees." At the polling stations, the pressure was immediate.

The ballot box sat on a rough table near the doorway, its presence both symbolic and absurd. There were no permanent walls, only timber frames and stretched canvas meant to suggest civic space.

Ben had arrived at the polling place with his father. He was too young to understand the law, but knew when adults were afraid. He stayed close to his father's pant leg, watching the boots, spurs, and pistols at belts. The air smelled of tobacco, sweat, and horses. Voices rose and fell above him.

Around them gathered settlers whose power to vote had become a matter of argument rather than a legal right. Some had arrived weeks earlier. Others had come across the Missouri River that very morning, armed with the certainty that participation justified itself. Large groups assembled together, voted, and then left. Residency requirements were ignored. The local authorities, when they resisted, were pushed aside.

"You don't belong here."

"This is free soil."

"We will decide our own future."

Words hardened into positions. Positions into threats.

To Ben, the words meant little, but the tone was understood. He watched one man jab a finger into another's chest. Nearby, rifles appeared from wagon beds where they had been stored as a precaution. He saw hands drift toward pistol grips and then away again.

His father, H.D., watched from the edge of the crowd, measuring the scene with the practiced caution of someone who knew how quickly conflict could erupt into violence. This election mattered. It would determine not only political allegiance but also security, investment confidence, and the survival of places still balancing on the edge of speculation.

Fear transformed the atmosphere. Judges were warned, and some were threatened outright. In a few cases, they were told they would be killed if they refused to give out ballots. Lines formed quickly, but they were not the lines the law had intended. Residents watched as men they did not know cast votes in their towns. Some stayed away entirely, unwilling to test how far the intimidation would go. Some retreated toward the river while others pressed forward, convinced that backing down would forfeit claims they had risked everything to assert. The idea that voting might be decided by force did not shock them entirely.

The phrase Bleeding Kansas gained traction not because violence was unprecedented, but because it now seemed inseparable from the project of settlement itself.

Ben saw mothers pull children back by the wrists and hurry indoors. He watched a dog slink beneath a wagon. He saw a man spit in the dirt and someone else kick over a crate in anger.

"Stay close now, Ben," his father instructed.

"Why are there so many men?"

"They've come for the voting," he stated matter of factly.

Ben was curious. "Do they live here?"

H.D. glanced toward the road before answering. "Some do. Some don't. Nothing to concern yourself with."

"Why has that man got a gun?"

"Because some men bring fear where reason would do."

"Are we going home soon?"

"When it's finished."

Suddenly, shouts rose near the doorway:

"Ben, behind me."

Ben complied, but now he just wanted to go home.

That night, lanterns burned late. People spoke in lowered voices about patrols and about the need to demonstrate strength without inviting escalation. The ballot box still rested where it had been placed, a simple artifact of governance where authority now traveled by rumor and rifle. A reminder that the future of Kansas — and perhaps the nation — would be determined not only by ideals but by whoever proved willing to defend them.

The town did not sleep easily.

Summer 1859 — Topeka, Kansas
Jennie Marie Safford, age 7

THEY HAD BEEN MOVING for weeks. Not traveling in the way people later would—by timetable, by rail, by anything predictable—but inching forward, mile by mile, across a country that was still in the process of becoming one. What had begun in Michigan as a decision had turned into a test of endurance.

The plains stretched out before them as it had for centuries before: vast and motionless except for the winter grasses bending in long ripples beneath a hard blue sky so wide it seemed to swallow the horizon whole. Here and there, the ground broke into streaks of rust-red earth and patches of sage, making the earth look at once barren and endlessly alive.

The covered wagon held everything. Tools, quilts, barrels of flour, and salt pork. What could not be packed was left behind. There was no room for sentiment when every pound became the enemy. Every hill and every expanse of mud reminded them of that.

Seven-year-old Jennie knew that this was not temporary. Four-year-old Endora was restless and asking questions that no one could answer to her satisfaction. Two-year-old Mary was too young to grasp anything beyond the steady rhythm of motion.

The days settled into repetition. Wake early. Break what little camp there was. Move. The wheels creaked constantly, wood against iron, a sound that became so familiar it disappeared into the background of thought. Where roads existed at all, they were little more than rutted, unreliable suggestions, cut into the prairie by the wheels and hooves of those who had gone west before them.

River crossings slowed everything. Weather decided progress more than intention did. A stretch of rain could hold them down for days, the ground turning and swallowing the wheels and exhausted animals. Dry days were no easier—dust coated everything, settled into clothes, into food, into lungs.

Other wagons appeared and disappeared along the way. Some traveling in loose company for safety. Some alone. Faces seen once and never again. Stories exchanged briefly at a stop—where they had come from, what they had heard about Kansas, how much land could be claimed when they got there.

Illustration, Family in Covered Wagon

Always the same question beneath it all: was it worth it?

They crossed into Illinois, then Missouri; the terrain widening, flattening, opening into ground that felt less settled with each passing mile. Towns grew farther apart. Supplies had to be managed carefully now. There was no easy replacement for what was used or lost. Time stretched. Three weeks. Now four. Closer to six when they pushed into Kansas Territory.

By then, the travel had changed them.

The children were quieter. Even Endora's questions had slowed, replaced by grueling stretches of watching the skyline or sleeping against her mother. The youngest had learned to endure discomfort without knowing why it was necessary. Jennie noticed things—how tired her parents were, how decisions seemed heavier, and how there was no turning back without cost. Esther, their mother, bore the uncertainty they wouldn't name aloud. The knowledge that this move — this long, grinding passage west — was not just about land or opportunity, but about survival, about starting again in a place that had not yet decided what it would be.

Kansas in 1859 was not settled, but contested. It was still raw and shaped by the violence of the years just before. Bleeding Kansas was not distant memory, but recent fact, and any offer of a homestead came with the reality of that instability.

And then, finally, Topeka. But it did not appear as a finished town. It emerged slowly, a scattering of hastily assembled buildings. Rough structures. Smoke rising from a handful of chimneys. Wagons, horses, and people moving with purpose, but no order of an established place. This was not an arrival into comfort. It was arrival into physical labor.

The wagon slowed as they entered. After weeks of constant motion, the stillness felt strange. The wheels stopped turning. The creak of wood and iron fell silent. For a moment, no one moved.

There was no ceremony to mark their arrival. Only the realization that it had led not to an end — but to the beginning of something far harder.

❖

THREE MOMENTS. THREE LIVES. One century of movement that would eventually converge. Billy Stealy was barely 15 years old when he stood on a battlefield alongside men who would die before sunset. Ben McMeekin's family claimed ground in a territory where every acre was a vote, every neighbor a potential enemy. Jennie Safford arrived in Topeka after weeks of grinding travel over the prairie.

The forces that had moved them – the hunger that emptied Ireland, the reforms that relocated children, and the expansion that promised land to anyone willing to fight for it – were larger than any of them. The intersection of these trajectories have been moving toward one another for decades.

One line arrives through pressure: Ireland. New York. Institutions. A farm. War. The other through expansion. The railroads. Civic structure. Town-building.

They do not meet as equals in experience, but they meet inside the same system. The lives that follow are both universal and distinctly American. They, like all of us, are travelers and refugees. Our ancestors have been blown off course for one reason or another. They faced economic pressures, social boundaries, and moments when the ground beneath them shifted. And when it does, they do what people have always done. They move. Not out of restlessness alone, but necessity. When the fields fail, when opportunity narrows, and when staying becomes harder than leaving, movement becomes the answer.

Migration and mobility are uniquely human; we are a curious species. We are drawn to explore and expand. It is the same impulse that propels people to cross oceans, borders, and generations. As I have reflected on their choices and decisions, I often wonder: how did they find the courage to start over, generation after generation? Building entire communities and lives from scratch. Would I have done the same?

It starts with my paternal grandmother, Jane Chamberlain, who was born in 1916 in Coronado, California. Her parents—

Lawrence Safford Chamberlain and Mabel Power—were well-established figures in a community that was itself still taking form along the edge of the Pacific. But, like everyone else in California at the time, their story did not begin there either.

Mabel's grandfather, William "Billy" Stealy, was born in Manhattan in the 1840s, the son of Irish immigrants who arrived to hardship rather than opportunity. Instability, density, and survival defined his early childhood in a city straining under the pressure of unending arrivals. He would not remain there. Like many of his generation, larger forces pushed him west: labor, war, and the constant search for footing in a country still expanding. He did not live long, but he built something that endured: a family line that would continue to move, adapt, and take root through decades.

Lawrence Safford Chamberlain came from a different current of that same movement. He was the son of Ben McMeekin and Jennie Safford, families shaped by earlier waves of American expansion. The McMeekins traced back through a sea of movement along the eastern seaboard—out of Delaware's Quaker communities, into Kentucky, and onward into Kansas. Their movements were not a single event, but a pattern: land, opportunity, pressure, and the steady push west. They were part of the population that did not simply witness the making of places like Kansas—they helped define them.

To understand what they became, we must first understand where they began. The stories that follow return to those beginnings—before Coronado, before California, before stability—back to the moments when each life was still uncertain, and everything that came after had yet to be decided.

2

The Stealy Family

Ireland, 1838

THE FIRST SIGN WAS the smell. Patrick Stealy noticed it while turning the soil with a borrowed spade, working a narrow strip of ground that had sustained his ancestors for as long as anyone could remember. At first, he thought an animal had died nearby, but the scent rose faintly from the earth itself — sour, wet, wrong.

When he unearthed the potatoes, they dissolved in his hands.

Only weeks earlier, they had stood green and promising. He had moved along the narrow rows, the plants already taller than they'd been a week before. Their leaves rustled against his legs as he passed, heavy with the assurance of a good harvest. He knew those buried treasures would feed his family through one more winter. He had never known anything else to depend on. Children grew strong on it. Families expanded. Rent could be paid, if barely. Survival was precarious but manageable.

Now what came away in his fingers was pulp—a softness that should have been flesh. He held it up to the light, already knowing what the smell meant. Around him, his

13

neighbors moved through their own plots in growing silence. The discovery did not need announcement. A failed crop was a failed crop, and it would travel from field to field without words. The precarious foundation of that balance was collapsing.

Like countless Catholic tenants in Ulster, he was not a landowner. He farmed ground controlled by distant Protestant landlords. When harvests failed, evictions followed with brutal efficiency. The blight did not come once and pass. It returned the following year, and the year after that.

Each season brought renewed hope that the disease might loosen its grip, only to be followed by fresh devastation as fields that had appeared healthy in summer succumbed to decay before winter stores could be secured. Livestock was sold to meet rent. Tools were pawned. Families crowded together, stretching dwindling resources across too many mouths. Hunger thinned faces and shortened tempers. It sent young men walking miles in search of day labor that might not exist. Fever followed want.

Patrick watched the world he knew disappear. He was in his late twenties when the crisis deepened into catastrophe. Old enough to recognize patterns and young enough to believe that action still mattered. Stories began circulating about America — wages higher than any available in Ireland, property that could be owned rather than rented, and cities where opportunity waited for those willing to endure the journey. No one described the voyage as easy.

The passage would cost more than most families could spare. Ships were crowded beyond reason, and illness claimed countless lives before land was sighted. But remaining meant something equally dangerous: accepting that survival might no longer be possible in the only place he had ever known. He made his decision.

Illustration, Ireland Famine, Public Domain.

MY THIRD GREAT-GRANDFATHER, Patrick Stealy, was born around 1816 in Ulster. The countryside of his youth, with its fields, hedgerows, and narrow lanes, was a product of generations of toil. Whether they held even a small tenancy or worked as hired hands is unknown. Regardless, their days were spent planting, cutting turf, tending animals, and enduring unreliable harvests. Days started early, dictated by light and weather. Work was constant. A man walked the same paths his father and grandfather had walked before him.

Labor was shared among everyone. Women balanced fieldwork with domestic responsibilities: baking bread, churning butter, mending clothing, and managing whatever resources they possessed. Children contributed from a young age, learning by doing rather than through formal schooling.

Their home would have been modest, built of rough stone or packed earth, with thatched roofs and low doorways. Inside, space was limited and communal. The main room was kitchen, workspace, and sleeping area. Families used pallet beds of straw or rushes laid on the floor at night and rolled away during the day. Children slept together, sometimes several to a bed, while parents occupied the most sheltered corner of the room. Furniture was sparse: a rough table, a few stools, perhaps a chest.

Light came from the hearth, which was also the center of domestic life — for cooking, conversation, and the mundane routines that structured each day. Cleanliness was maintained as best as possible, but the boundary between indoors and outdoors was thin, especially in wet seasons when mud was tracked in on boots and tools.

But when Patrick was coming of age in the 1830s, this rural world was under strain. Ulster found itself in an era of heightened sectarian conflict, partly due to Catholic Emancipation in 1829. Old religious tensions hardened, and secret groups asserted themselves. Faith was not simply a personal belief; it was identity, politics, and economic position.

At the same time, Catholic tenants, forced to pay tithes to the Anglican Church, and for families living close to subsistence, these payments were deeply resented. They resisted. This period was known as the Tithe War. For Patrick, stability must have felt increasingly out of reach.

The earth still structured daily subsistence, but it no longer guaranteed permanence. Everything pressed inward at once. The house with its pallet beds was quickly becoming a place where limits were becoming clear.

Illustration, Irish Family c 1840

Sometime in his early twenties, Patrick met Mary Deegan, another Catholic from his village. Their marriage, around 1836, was both personal and practical. Rural Irish marriages of the era were rarely built on romance alone. They were alliances against hardship—two people binding themselves to shared labor, shared risk, and the daily uncertainty of a world that offered little stability. Husband and wife needed one another in practical, immediate ways: fields to plow, children to raise, illness to endure, and winters to survive. Marriage was often less a private sentiment than a mutual strategy for staying upright in a precarious world.

For a few brief years, they lived inside that older world. Their hopes were modest: to keep a roof over their heads, see their children grow strong, and perhaps secure better land.

By the late 1830s, population growth had further strained resources. Agricultural changes and tightening landlord expectations made long-term security untenable. Their decision to leave would have emerged gradually, as conversations repeated themselves around hearths and at parish gatherings. People told stories about wages in America and about cities with available work.

"They say a man can earn coin every week in New York."

"They say many things."

"Aye, but they say there is work there."

"And here?"

"Here there is rent."

Another voice, quieter than the rest: "If we wait until we must go, we'll go with nothing."

And so they made their decision. They were not yet part of the catastrophic refugee waves of the later 1840s, but among the earlier strivers — immigrants who bet on America while conditions at home were tightening.

On 24 December 1839, Patrick and Mary made their way to Liverpool, the most practical gateway to America, and boarded the ship *Rochester*, bound for New York. They departed not as adventure seekers but as witnesses to the collapse of a system that had kept them one failed harvest away from ruin. The ship's manifest preserves the date, but I wonder what they felt as the coastline receded.

The Voyage

An Atlantic crossing in 1839 was a challenging undertaking. Patrick and Mary would have traveled in steerage, the lowest and cheapest class aboard. The crossing typically took five to eight weeks, depending on winds, storms, and the ship's condition. But winter crossings, like theirs, could be especially brutal. North Atlantic gales slowed progress and made conditions below deck miserable.

Passengers slept in tightly packed wooden berths, often stacked in tiers. Ventilation was poor. Food was basic and sometimes spoiled: salted meat, ship's biscuit, porridge, and tea when available. Fresh water was rationed. Seasickness was constant in heavy weather, and illness could spread quickly in the confined air. Families cooked for themselves on shared galley stoves when the weather permitted; during storms, they might eat cold leftovers for days.

But even in these conditions, the voyage must have had an unmistakable emotional charge. Fellow travelers clustered together on deck when seas were calm, scanning the horizon and sharing tales of what awaited them in America: wages, stability, and the chance to live beyond the limits of the old country. For Patrick and Mary, traveling together meant facing the unknown as a unit, a married couple stepping into a future neither could imagine.

When the *Rochester* finally entered New York Harbor, Manhattan was booming. Sailing ships crowded the waterfront, and warehouses, shipyards, and tenements pressed against each other. The possibilities of opportunity were immediately matched by the reality of competition and density. It must have been overwhelming.

Illustration, New York Harbor, 1840

Manhattan, New York — 1840

For Patrick, there was no gentle introduction to American life. New York simply absorbed them. They had to immediately find work and a place to stay. Survival depended on joining networks of kin or fellow countrymen who had arrived earlier and learned how to navigate the new order. Their future would be built day by day, with little margin for failure.

Patrick first took whatever work he could find near the docks or in the expanding commercial districts — unloading cargo, carrying goods, or performing day labor while he learned the rhythms of the American marketplace. Mary's labor was no less essential. In crowded boarding houses or rented rooms, she would have taken in washing, sewing, or domestic service to supplement the household income. Together, they navigated an environment that was both harsh and full of possibility, where advancement depended as much on endurance as on opportunity.

The record of their experience is sparse. Like most immigrant families of modest means, Patrick and Mary left few written traces behind—no deeds in their names, no newspaper notices, no surviving letters to mark their struggles or milestones. Only a handful of records remain to suggest what came next.

"Irish Need Not Apply"

When they arrived in America, the Irish were viewed with suspicion and resentment. Immigration from Ireland had been steadily increasing for years, and in cities like New

York, the population was becoming visible in ways that unsettled the native-born residents. The era marked a broader cultural anxiety about rapid urban growth, changing labor markets, and religious differences. The prejudice they would have encountered was not always dramatic or violent; often it operated more quietly — in hiring decisions, social exclusion, assumptions about character, and the limits placed on how far an immigrant might realistically rise.

Religion lay at the center of this tension. Most were Catholic in a nation that defined itself culturally and politically through Protestant norms. Many Americans believed Catholicism was inherently incompatible with republican government. Sermons, broadsheets, and political speeches warned that Irish immigrants would vote as a bloc under clerical influence, threatening democratic independence. Even when Irish migrants demonstrated motivation and discipline, they were often viewed through this lens of suspicion.

Economic fear intensified these attitudes. New York in the 1840s was transforming into a commercial powerhouse. Canals, railroads, shipping networks, and manufacturing were reshaping opportunity — but also creating intense competition. Immigrants frequently took low wages and accepted difficult jobs because they had few alternatives. To native residents, this made them both indispensable and resented. They were seen as undercutting established labor standards while simultaneously filling roles essential to the labor market's growth.

Cultural stereotypes only reinforced the divide. Popular cartoons and editorials portrayed Irish men as volatile or intemperate, their neighborhoods as disorderly, and Irish families as perpetually on the edge of poverty. Such images simplified complex realities but shaped everyday perception. Respectability needed to be constantly demonstrated and defended. A man like Patrick, seeking advancement in retail trade, would have understood that his conduct, speech, and reliability were not merely personal traits — they were tests of belonging.

Cartoon depicting the Irish, Public Domain.

By the late 1840s and early 1850s, these sentiments hardened into organized political movements that openly sought to restrict immigrants' influence. Patrick lived at the threshold of this escalation. The prejudice was real and persistent, but not yet fully institutionalized. This created a narrow window in which determined individuals could move cautiously upward before barriers became more rigid.

Sometime during this unsettled decade, their family grew. A son, Thomas, was born around 1834; a daughter, Mary, followed several years later, and finally William, whom they called Billy, around 1842. Children have a way of anchoring people more firmly than occupation alone. Decisions that might once have been temporary became permanent. Neighborhood ties formed. Work connections deepened. The dream of returning to Ireland, if it had ever been seriously entertained, gradually receded.

In the 1850 United States Census, Patrick Stealy had carved out a modest foothold in this new world. He was listed as age thirty and employed as a clerk in retail trade, a position that suggests literacy, numeracy, and a measure of trust earned over years of steady effort. The Stealys were living in New York's Fourteenth Ward, one of the dense immigrant districts of lower Manhattan, where commerce, poverty, drive, and survival existed side by side.

Ward 14

Immigrant communities formed quickly in the lower districts of Manhattan. The Fourteenth Ward of Manhattan was part of the dense lower-neighborhood shaped by commerce and constant activity. It lay inside the expanding grid that would later include the notorious Five Points area and surrounding streets. It was a patchwork of boarding houses, general stores, workshops, and crowded tenements. Streets were muddy, narrow, and uneven. Livestock could still be seen moving through the lanes alongside drays and handcarts. Here, accents were familiar, but conditions were not. Employment might come one day on the docks, the next hauling materials for construction, the next not at all. Earnings vanished quickly into food, lodging, and the small remittances some still tried to send home.

Buildings rose close together, often housing multiple families in subdivided rooms or converted boarding arrangements. Sanitation and health conditions were precarious. Open drains, unreliable water supply, and overcrowding contributed to periodic outbreaks of disease. Entire households often occupied spaces barely large enough for sleeping. Shared water pumps and privies served dozens of residents. Waste collected in gutters and disease traveled easily through crowded stairwells.

Noise was constant: carts delivering goods from the docks, street vendors advertising wares, and children playing in whatever open space could be found. But the ward also held opportunity. Its closeness to the waterfront and commercial streets meant work could be found nearby. Shops, stockrooms, and growing manufacturing facilities created a local economy that rewarded persistence and adaptability.

Retail trade — Patrick's line of work — was one of the most accessible ladders for advancement for those with basic literacy or numeracy. Clerks kept account books, managed inventory, assisted customers, and sometimes lived above or near the shop. This role suggests Patrick had progressed beyond day labor into a slightly more stable and respectable position within the urban economy.

This was not a purely Irish district. Germans, native-born Americans, and migrants from other regions of Europe lived alongside Irish families, creating a patchwork of languages and customs. Neighborhoods revolved around parish churches, taverns, local markets, and workplaces that doubled as social centers. Mutual aid societies and informal networks helped newcomers find employment or lodging, but they also reinforced ethnic boundaries.

New York Street, Illustration, 1840

Yet these tenements were also communities. Doors were left open when the weather allowed. Women exchanged

26

gossip and news while preparing meals. Children roamed freely between rooms, forming bonds that blurred the lines between family and neighbor. Kinship groups mattered. A cousin might provide temporary lodging. An aunt might help care for a newborn. Survival depended on cooperation as much as endurance.

For Patrick and Mary, living in Ward 14 meant accepting a tradeoff common to immigrant families: proximity to employment at the cost of comfort. It was a place to begin, not necessarily a place to remain forever — though many did.

❖

MORNING CAME EARLY IN Ward 14. Patrick Stealy woke before the light had fully pushed its way between the narrow buildings. The room was warm with breath and closeness. Someone downstairs was already moving — boots on plank floors, the scrape of a chair. From the street came the familiar low thunder of carts beginning their day. He lay still for a moment, listening. The air smelled of damp wood and last night's coal smoke.

Mary was up. He could hear the quiet rhythm of her working near the window — folding clothing, imposing domestic order on rooms that never seemed meant for living. Their younger children still slept, curled against the wall. Thomas had gone early to whatever errand or apprenticeship he now kept; boys in this city became men quickly.

Patrick dressed silently. His clothes were neat but worn: dark trousers brushed free of lint, a waistcoat mended twice at the pocket seam. A clerk's respectability depended on appearances. He washed at the basin with water that had lost its chill overnight, ran his hand once over his hair, and took the small ledger he sometimes studied at home — figures he meant to master. Outside, the street was alive.

New York City did not ease into the morning; it lunged. Vendors shouted in accents that overlapped and collided — Irish, German, and English. Horses snorted clouds into the cool air. A drayman cursed as he maneuvered his load past a heap of refuse not yet hauled away. Somewhere nearby, a child cried without interruption. The smell was a mixture he had stopped trying to separate: brine from the river, rotting vegetables, wet rope, human density.

He walked quickly. Clerks were expected before the doors opened. The shop stood on a commercial street not far from the waterfront — a narrow frontage crowded between a warehouse importer and a tobacconist. The windows displayed bolts of cloth and finished goods: handkerchiefs, ribbons, combs, inexpensive luxuries for people who still wished to feel respectable. Inside, the owner was there, unlocking the iron cash drawer with a practiced turn. Patrick nodded, hung his coat, and took his position behind the counter.

The morning hours belonged to accounts. He sharpened a quill and bent over the tall book, columns ruled in carmine ink. Numbers had become his language of survival. He noted deliveries, tallied the previous day's sales, and copied invoices written in a hand more elegant than his own. Precision mattered. A mistake could mean reprimand, dismissal, or replacement by one of the dozens of young men who hovered constantly at the edge of opportunity.

When the door opened, work became performance. Customers stepped in carrying the streets with them — dust on heels and worry on their faces. A seamstress needing thread on credit, and a dock laborer's wife bargaining hard for a length of cheap wool.

"I'll pay you Saturday, Mr. Stealy. You know I will."

Patrick responded, "Aye, Mrs. Donnelly. Then take the thread now and keep your word later."

Another customer held up a bolt of cloth between finger and thumb. "That's thin enough to see daylight through."

"It's thin enough to fit the purse you brought in," Patrick replied, not unkindly. "But I've a sturdier piece if you've another quarter hidden somewhere."

She almost smiled. "If I had another shilling to my name—or a quarter besides—I'd hide it from you first."

Patrick operated easily among them now. He had learned how to listen, how to flatter without seeming to, how to judge what someone could truly afford. He wrapped purchases in brown paper, tied them with string, and slid them across the counter with a slight inclination of the head.

At midday, he ate standing up. Bread, cheese, perhaps a bit of salted meat if the week had gone well. He stepped outside briefly, letting the river air strike his face. Masts crowded the skyline like a forest. Ships came and went with purpose, carrying away and bringing in thousands of lives like his own. Then he went back to the shop and its ledger.

Afternoon blurred into evening. The gas lamps were lit early in the winter months; their yellow glow and his fatigue flattened everything. His fingers grew stained with ink, and his back ached from standing. Still, he stayed focused, careful, and balanced the books. When at last the shutters were drawn, Patrick stepped into the night that was scarcely different from day.

Ward 14 never truly slept. Music spilled from a nearby tavern. Somewhere a fight had begun — the dull, rhythmic sound of bodies striking. He kept his eyes forward. The walk home was slower.

Mary's days in New York required a different kind of strength. While men navigated the fluctuations of wage labor, women often bore the burden of maintaining stability amid instability. Meals had to be prepared from limited supplies. Clothing repaired and reused. Children supervised in environments where danger was never far away — from traffic, from illness, from the simple hazards of overcrowded living. Mary's world revolved around making scarcity manageable.

She had risen early, organizing the day around tasks that rarely earned recognition but ensured survival. Water fetched. Floors swept. Food stretched. Infant and child mortality remained high, and mothers lived with the constant awareness that love alone could not guarantee protection.

In their rented room above the street, Mary managed to coax a meal into existence. Their daughter proudly showed them her schoolwork, beaming with pride at the letters she had learned to write. Thomas spoke of work, wages, and the future as if they were already within his reach.

"There's money to be made there, if a man is willing."

"And who says so?" asked Patrick.

"The men at the docks."

"Men boast cheaply. And if there's no work?"

Thomas smiled faintly. "Then I'll find where it is."

Patrick listened more than he spoke, envious of the certainty of youth. Manhattan pressed in on him from all sides, but here — in this narrow space claimed at great cost — he could briefly believe that the gamble had been worth it.

Illustration of a Typical Room in Ward 14, New York c 1850s

Before sleep, he lay again in darkness. Through the thin walls, he heard strangers breathing, coughing, living. Beyond them, the river ran invisibly in the night. Somewhere out there, ships still traversed the Atlantic as his had once done, carrying them toward the same tentative hope. He closed his eyes, knowing that morning would come quickly. But for a moment, he allowed himself to imagine advancement — a partnership, maybe his own shop one day, and a safer street for the children.

In that crowded ward, they had achieved what would have seemed doubtful when they first stepped ashore a decade earlier: they had endured. The record of their lives is brief—a census ledger, a date, and a location. But it captures ten formative years: the time they remade their future in a metropolis that demanded everything and offered just enough.

Thomas, at sixteen, would soon enter the workforce, contributing to the household economy. The younger children, Mary and Billy, represented the second generation — children whose formative years were shaped not by Ireland but by the rhythms and pressures of urbanization. Faith, community ties, and shared cultural traditions offered continuity with the world left behind. Church bells marked time. Irish songs and stories survived in whispered recollections. Even in the harshest circumstances, people sought ways to believe that the next generation might live more securely than the last. But the problem of insecurity wasn't solved, only transferred from rural to urban. From famine to labor. From one form of uncertainty to another.

Within a year, Patrick would be dead. Mary would be dead, and young Billy would be left an orphan in an indifferent city.

❖

MARY STEALY'S DEATH IS recorded only in the barest terms. On February 22, 1851, she died in New York City at Bellevue Hospital, leaving behind no surviving explanation of what illness or injury brought her there. Like so many immigrant urban lives in the mid-nineteenth century, the details that must have filled her last days — the fear, the physical suffering, the anxious waiting of family — were never written down. What remains is a location, a date, and the knowledge that her life ended in an institution for the sick and the poor.

Bellevue stood at the edge of the East River, and by the early 1850s, it had become the primary municipal hospital for those who could not afford private care. Patients arrived there by wagon, by boat, or on foot, often only when illness had progressed beyond easy remedy. The hospital's wards were large and austere. Rows of iron bedsteads lined narrow rooms where nurses and physicians went quickly from patient to patient, operating with limited tools and an incomplete understanding of disease.

For Mary, admission to Bellevue likely meant that her condition had worsened to the point that care at home was no longer possible. Patrick would have depended heavily on neighbors during her illness, but the demands of daily survival would have made prolonged nursing difficult. Sending her to the hospital was not a decision he made lightly. It represented both hope — that professional treatment might succeed — and an acknowledgment of their vulnerability.

In the winter of 1851, New York was still learning to manage public health. Only two years earlier, the city had endured one of the most frightening public health crises of the era. In 1849, a major cholera outbreak arrived, exposing just how vulnerable immigrant neighborhoods were to disease. Cholera spread through contaminated water — a constant danger in lower Manhattan, where overcrowded tenements relied on shallow wells, shared pumps, and open drains. Waste disposal was primitive, and clean drinking water was never guaranteed.

The epidemic tore quickly through dense wards. Entire streets became sites of sudden loss. Households fell ill within days. The papers shared daily death counts, and fear was part of everyday existence. Malnutrition, exhaustion, and the stress of urban living weakened immigrants' resistance to illness. Without antibiotics or modern diagnostic methods, physicians could offer little more than observation, basic remedies, and comfort.

The outbreak weakened confidence in its ability to protect its residents and left lasting health consequences for some survivors. It also revealed how precarious the gains of immigrant families could be. Years of careful effort — securing work, stabilizing a household, raising children — could be undone by forces beyond their control.

When Mary was admitted to Bellevue, public health reforms were being discussed, but had not yet transformed the crowded wards. Her cause of death is unknown. Only that it happened in a nation that was only beginning to understand how environment, poverty, and disease intertwined.

Mary's death would have reverberated deeply in the household. She had kept their fragile lives from falling apart. Now her absence created not only emotional loss but practical uncertainty. Who would manage the daily effort of maintaining the home? Who would guide the younger children through an unforgiving world? For Patrick, the loss would have been catastrophic.

Thomas was almost certainly working by now. He may have been employed as a delivery boy, warehouse helper, apprentice, or shop assistant, moving goods through the same crowded streets where his father worked at the counter. Such labor was rarely secure or well-paid, but it was a necessary step toward manhood and his own survival.

For the younger children, Mary and Billy, childhood would have narrowed quickly. At nine and ten, they took on responsibilities that we would find startling today, but were entirely typical for the era. Children ran errands for shopkeepers, minded younger boarders' children, sorted scraps in workshops, or helped with piecework that they could do at home.

But they were not entirely alone. Neighbors, fellow parishioners, and extended networks of countrymen would have stepped in when a family suffered loss. Patrick would have relied on the women in adjoining rooms to supervise the younger children during working hours. Older youths watched younger ones. Meals would have been brought or shared when resources allowed. These arrangements were rarely documented but formed the invisible safety net that enabled families to endure.

For Patrick, grief had to be balanced against the relentless demands of employment. Expenses continued. His position required reliability and composure, and every minute away from the shop risked dismissal. Each day, he labored at the counter while the household adjusted, imperfectly, to a new reality. Another illness, unemployment, or a single misfortune could tip the now precarious balance.

By the autumn of 1852, Patrick Stealy had been in New York for nearly thirteen years. He had endured prejudice, the work of building a household, and the devastating loss of his wife. Then, on September 26, there is a brief, final entry.

He died at thirty-six, the cause noted simply as epilepsy — a word that in that era often meant sudden collapse, convulsions, and little understanding. In the dense streets around 121 Cedar Street, where illness spread quickly, and medical certainty was rare, a life could end with nothing more than a line in a register.

He had arrived as part of a larger human tide — one of hundreds of thousands moved across the Atlantic by necessity more than hope. He died abruptly and was almost certainly laid to rest among the numerous anonymous dead, without a marker or lasting remembrance. Two young children were now left behind, and their lives would be permanently changed.

3

The McMeekin Family

WHILE THE STEALY FAMILY was enduring loss and upheaval, another set of forces was silently shaping the family whose path would one day converge with theirs.

This branch of our roots lay in the eastern colonies, among the Quaker-influenced communities of Delaware and the Tidewater fringes of Virginia. They were among the first to move deeper into the country after the Revolution. These were not frontier people yet, but participants still rooted in an older world—structured, agricultural, and tied to the Atlantic economy. Like many families who would shape the early West, they had migrated there in stages—out of the original colonies, through Kentucky, and finally into the disputed ground of Kansas Territory.

Benjamin McMeekin was born into this second wave of movement. He was Kentucky-born, but already part of a line that did not stay in one place for long. It was his father, Hayden D. "H.D." McMeekin, who had pushed them into the Kansas frontier.

MY IMMIGRANT ANCESTOR, WILLIAM McMechen (the spelling would change several times in the following decades), arrived in the Delaware colony in 1720, not as a marginal settler but as a member of an organized passage of roughly sixty individuals from Armagh, Northern Ireland, and part of the larger Scots-Irish movement into the American colonies. Drawn by the promise of land, relative religious freedom, and the chance to establish permanence, he settled in New Castle, in what was then Pennsylvania (now Delaware), a region that was defined by William Penn's Quaker influence and emerging colonial structure.

This is where truth and memory begin to overlap. William married into the Claypooles, a connection preserved in family lore as the union between an Irish settler and an English "lady." They were prosperous, well-established, and respected within their community, part of a network of families shaped by the Society of Friends' long traditions of literacy, discipline, and civic responsibility. Quakers believed that every person carried an inner light—a direct spark of the divine—which challenged rigid hierarchies of class, race, and gender more than many nineteenth-century Americans were willing to admit. From that belief flowed practical habits: plain living, honesty in dealings, skepticism toward vanity, concern for the poor, and a deep commitment to reform causes, especially abolition and humane treatment of the vulnerable.

These communities also had long histories of antislavery activism, women's participation in public moral work, and organized charity. In such households, daughters were often educated seriously, expected to speak thoughtfully, and entrusted with responsibility uncommon in many neighboring cultures. Women were raised to be useful. The Quaker suspicion of empty display also bred a certain steadiness under pressure—less concern for ceremony, more concern for what needed doing immediately.

The Claypooles also possessed a noble heritage reaching into the English gentry, with direct links to King Edward I. Amazingly, this is true. Their lineage was one of prestige, acquired wealth, and integration into the colonial system. And they sought one thing in the new world: land.

From the beginning, the McMechens appear not at the margins, but inside that system. Their name appears repeatedly in early Delaware archives, tied to property purchases, transfers, and adjacency to other well-established families. They were not transient. They anchored themselves, expanded outward through landholding, and participated in the steady consolidation of colonial settlement. Parcels were acquired, divided, transferred, and expanded—often near their extended family, suggesting not random arrangement but strategic growth. Property ownership in this period was not just economic—it was identity, stability, and political presence. Of course, however, it wasn't theirs.

The survey stakes that William McMechen drove into the ground still held the memory of Lenape fires. The Indigenous People, especially bands such as the Unami-speaking Lenape, whose villages, hunting grounds, and river corridors stretched over the Delaware Valley long before English deeds imposed their boundaries. The papers he carried—the grants and official licenses—were new. But the land was not. William did not think much about the difference. Few did. It was settlers like him who brought disease, forced displacement, unequal treaties, and colonial pressure. The legacy of colonization casts a long shadow.

During the American Revolution, the line—now spelled McMakin—moved south into Loudoun County, Virginia, placing them in one of the most active and economically significant regions of the colony. William McMechen's grandson was Major Alexander McMakin, a merchant and participant in the struggle for American independence. His mercantile offered him a position of steady influence. He was not simply selling goods across a counter. He was extending credit, managing supplies, and serving as a node in a wider economic network that connected local farmers to the Atlantic trade. His store in Leesburg sold imported goods—cloth, tools, salt, and ironware—items that could not be produced locally. But more importantly, he would have sold much of it on account.

Cash was scarce. Trust was currency. Customers took what they needed and paid later—after harvest, after livestock sales, after conditions allowed. Which meant a merchant like Alexander McMakin was part shopkeeper, part lender, and part enforcer of obligation. He even occasionally sued customers to recover debts, a common practice that reveals both the system's fragility and his role within it. He was not peripheral. He was necessary.

By 1770, he lived on a tract called "Cocke's Patent," just south of Leesburg—an asset that further anchored his status. Property, commerce, and credit were intertwined. He held all three.

Artist Rendering, Alexander McMakin

He also married into another established colonial line—
one that extended back to the early Dutch colony of New
Amsterdam in the seventeenth century. Like earlier
marriage alliances, this was not incidental. It reinforced
position, connection, and continuity in a society where
networks determined opportunity.

When war came, men like Alexander did not stand apart
from it. They organized it. By 1777, he was serving as an
officer in the Third Battalion of the Loudoun County Militia,
with his own son under his command. This was not
symbolic service. Militia officers were responsible for
recruitment, readiness, and, quite commonly, financing. On
March 13, 1781, he was promoted from Captain to Major—a
rank that placed him in a position of real authority within
the county's military structure. But his service came at a cost
that would follow him.

In 1779, Virginia required militia captains to contribute financially to enlistment bounties—cash payments used to secure soldiers. The incentive was straightforward: advance the money, and receive relief through a tax credit the following year.

Alexander did more than was required. He advanced nine hundred pounds—an enormous sum equivalent to more than $200,000 today—for two soldiers in his own company, and then funded two more for another captain who failed to meet the obligation. It was an act that combined patriotism, pressure, and expectation. The system depended on men like him stepping in.

The repayment never came.

Years later, in December of 1800, he petitioned the Virginia House of Delegates, laying out the account in precise terms: the money advanced, the offered credit, the failure of reimbursement. The sum still owed—£873—was substantial. He argued not from emotion, but from duty and obligation. The petition was denied.

Whether due to a lack of documentation, shifting standards, or simple bureaucratic indifference, the result was the same. The Commonwealth did not repay him. It is a minor moment in the Revolution's scale, but it reveals a larger truth: Alexander McMakin and those like him helped finance the war at a local level. They extended credit not only to neighbors, but to the emerging nation itself—often without guarantee of return. Their losses did not make it into the history books, but they were part of the real cost of independence.

By the end of his years, Alexander McMakin had occupied multiple roles: merchant, landholder, militia officer, and creditor to both individuals and the state.

After the Revolution, as families expanded, the previously claimed ground tightened around them. And, like thousands more, they went inland. Alexander McMakin's son, William, left Virginia and settled in Kentucky by the first decade of the nineteenth century, part of a broad resettlement that transformed the region into one of the first true gateways to the West. Kentucky was no longer the wilderness it had once been, but it was not settled ground either. It was in transition—where eastern customs met frontier realities, and where the next move west was always visible in the distance.

In 1806, William McMakin was among those pushing beyond the Appalachians into a region that offered scale, productivity, and permanence. But Kentucky was not Delaware. And it was not Virginia. It is harder—and more revealing. When he appears in Jefferson County, Virginia (now West Virginia) in 1810 and then firmly in Nelson County, Kentucky by 1820, the structure of his existence becomes visible. Numbers tell the story.

In 1810, his household included two enslaved people. By 1820, that number had expanded significantly—thirteen enslaved individuals living and working for his family. By 1830, that number had grown again. More than half of the people on his property are enslaved. The labor that sustains his land, his production, and his status is not his own, nor his family's. This is not incidental ownership. This is scale.

The language of the era reduces people to categories—age ranges, gender, and totals. This was not abstract participation in a system, but direct, daily dependence on it. Their names were not recorded.

Two males, 43

Female, 36

Female, 12

Female, 10

Male, 8

Male, 6

Male, 4

Male, 2

Male, 4 months

William McMakin is no longer operating within the looser systems of colonial commerce and landholding that defined earlier generations. The documents make this plain. Estate and tax lists indicate hundreds of acres under his control, and agricultural production required labor beyond what his household alone could provide. He is building an agricultural enterprise rooted in a slave economy, dependent on it and structured by it. His success relies on labor he does not pay, and cannot sustain without. So he acquired it.

Even the inventory of his estate points to a level of material possessions that set him apart from subsistence farmers—livestock in significant numbers, multiple structures, and household goods that signaled comfort rather than subsistence. The property he accumulated, the wealth he built, and the stability his family would inherit were dependent on the enslaved labor of others.

Discovering that the McMeekins enslaved other human beings was not the first time I found ancestors who owned slaves, nor would it be the last. But it was the first time ancestry became an encounter with moral inheritance. I had not done what they had done. However, some portion of the world I inherited may have been built from it. The question was not whether I could absolve them, but if I was willing to tell the truth.

Illustration of Kentucky Homestead

His choices matter because inheritance is not only property or money but also structure and worldview, and it is what a family comes to see as normal, necessary, and justified. The decisions he made in Kentucky did not remain in Kentucky. They were deposited into his children's memories, expectations, and beliefs. His children carried those ideas into Kansas, a territory where violence, not law or geography, settled the question of slavery. When that conflict emerges in Kansas, it will not be abstract for the McMeekin line. It will be inherited.

❖

HAYDEN D. MCMEEKIN—SIMPLY referred to as H.D.— was the grandson of William. The structure built by his ancestors in Kentucky did not end with one generation. His father, Charles, also held enslaved people, though on a smaller scale. The quantity shifted, but the foundation remained the same. What had been established as practice became expectation. Ownership and labor. Not debated— but assumed.

H.D. did not arrive at these ideas through theory or politics alone. He was raised inside them. They were part of the household, part of the economy, part of what it meant to build and maintain a livelihood. When he moves into the Kansas Territory, it is not neutral space. He entered at a time when the systems that had structured his worldview were being challenged openly. In law, in elections, and increasingly, in violence.

Through this era, the McMeekin line reveals a consistent pattern. They were not passive participants in American expansion, whether for good or bad. They were embedded in its systems—economic, social, and military—well before they ever reached the Kansas territory. The chapter that follows turns to that moment—when legacy becomes action, and private belief blends into public conflict. That place that would come to be known as Bleeding Kansas.

4

The Safford Family

———————————◄◆►———————————

JACOB SAFFORD, WHO WAS known in Kansas and in my family as "the Judge," belonged to a different phase of the frontier than the McMeekins. He arrived in Kansas when it was still volatile, establishing himself not as a laborer or settler, but as a man of law, infrastructure, and influence.

Born in Vermont in 1827, Jacob stood at the far edge of a lineage that reached back to the first fragile footholds of English colonization in New England. His family had moved in steady increments through generations—out of coastal Massachusetts, through Connecticut, and into the interior of Vermont—following the familiar pattern of opportunity and pressure that shaped early American expansion.

At the beginning of that line was Thomas Safford, who arrived in 1627 from the English coastal village of Seaford. He arrived in the colonies bringing with him a corporate seal from that village—a relic that suggests standing or responsibility, though its exact meaning has been lost to time. Whatever status he may have held in England mattered less than what he could build with his hands in Ipswich, Massachusetts.

In the 1640s, Ipswich stood inside the homeland of the Agawam people, a coastal Native community whose world had been profoundly disrupted by epidemic disease and the

first decades of English colonization. Before large numbers
of whites arrived, the Agawam and neighboring peoples
had sustained themselves through fishing, planting,
hunting, and seasonal travel across a landscape they knew
intimately. But waves of disease—likely introduced through
European contact—killed thousands and weakened the
social fabric that had ordered life for generations.

When English families arrived in larger numbers and
started to establish settlements along the Massachusetts
coast, they entered not an empty wilderness but a place
already shaped by Native labor, memory, and loss. Fields
had been cleared, paths worn into the land, fisheries known,
and boundaries understood, even if colonists rarely
recognized them on those terms. Trade, uneasy alliances,
land pressure, and cultural misunderstanding marked the
early decades that followed. In places like Ipswich, English
expansion advanced most easily where Native communities
had already been diminished, their reduced numbers
masking the depth of what had been taken.

It is unlikely that any of this weighed heavily on my
ancestors, or on the thousands of other white colonists who
settled on the eastern seaboard. They arrived with
assumptions common to their age: that land was theirs to
claim. In that sense, they carried an early version of Manifest
Destiny—a belief that expansion was natural, justified, even
ordained. And step by step, colonization advanced
accordingly.

Thomas Safford was a blacksmith by trade, a position of
importance in a world where ironwork meant survival—
tools, hinges, nails, repairs. But he did not remain a simple

tradesman. By February 8, 1648, he had begun to establish himself as a landholder, purchasing a 32-acre farm. That purchase was only the beginning. Over the following years, his holdings expanded to roughly sixty acres, a mix of workable fields and low, fertile ground. There was a house, barn, and a cider mill—evidence of stability, of a household rooted rather than transient. By 1664, he also held a share and a half in Plum Island, extending his interests beyond inland farming to the colony's coastal margins.

Illustration of the Cider Mill originally owned by John Safford

A surviving town plot from the late seventeenth century shows how the community was physically arranged. Safford's parcel was not an isolated holding, but a tightly ordered grid—thin, narrow house lots set along a common road, each designed to give access to fields, meadow, and water. Neighbors stood close by, their names recurring across deeds and boundaries. This was not wilderness, but a structured community, where proximity mattered, and ground was divided with intention. The pattern reflects a world in which survival depended not only on individual effort, but on being placed—deliberately—within a network.

This was the pattern that defined the Safford line: not sudden wealth or prominence, but accumulation—acreage added parcel by parcel, security built through their own labor, position earned gradually, year by year. With the birth of his grandson, Joseph Safford, in 1662, mobility reappears, and the family shifts from Massachusetts to Preston, Connecticut. They were counted among the steady inland push that characterized late seventeenth-century New England, where they remained for multiple generations, extending their foothold—felling trees, building households, and embedding themselves in a new community.

By the mid-eighteenth century, the demands on that kind of existence had changed. Property alone was no longer the only measure of obligation. Joseph's son, John Safford, stepped into a different role, serving as a lieutenant in Captain John Perkins' company during the French and Indian War. In August 1757, his unit was called out in response to the alarm surrounding Fort William Henry in the broader struggle between British and French forces for control of the northern borderlands. This was not distant war. It pressed directly against the edges of towns, pulling men like John from their farms into sudden service. The same family that had once measured its world in acres and boundary lines was now tied to a larger conflict—one that would reshape the colonies themselves.

By the late 1700s, the Safford line had settled in Preston, Connecticut, where another John Safford was born, who joined the push north into Vermont and became one of the early grantees at Royalton. It was a familiar decision: land newly available, risk balanced against opportunity, and a willingness to leave the familiar for what is not yet secured.

Royalton was completely raw terrain then, mostly forest, part town, and the rest speculation. John's son, Jacob, took up the ministry and was the Deacon of the First Church. The next generation became fixed in local governance when his son, another Jacob, was elected Town Clerk in 1805. He was also among those who helped establish the Oberlin colony in Ohio in the 1830s, a planned community built around shared religious and reformist ideals.

Jacob "Johnson" Safford, as he was called, so as not to confuse him with his son, Jacob Jr, was not only present in Oberlin's earliest days, clear-cutting trees, helping shape the village, and taking part in its civic underpinnings, but was pushing it into something more morally ambitious. Oberlin was not simply another frontier settlement. It was a community built on conviction. In 1845, his name appears in the student lists at Oberlin College, placing him in one of the most forward-looking institutions in the country.

Oberlin

Founded in the 1830s, it quickly emerged as one of the most openly abolitionist areas in the country, where religious belief and social change were inseparable. The town and its college admitted Black students and women when most academies refused both. Oberlin was a community defined by moral choice, and its residents were not passive observers of the slavery issue. They acted.

Oberlin was a well-known stop on the Underground Railroad, where those fleeing bondage could find shelter, assistance, and, when possible, protection in defiance of federal law. That defiance was not theoretical. In 1858, townspeople participated in the Oberlin-Wellington Rescue, forcibly freeing a captured fugitive and sending him onward to Canada rather than see him returned to slavery.

The school's ethos was clear: slavery was a moral wrong that demanded action. It was argued in absolutes: freedom and bondage, complicity and resistance. Students were expected to choose a position and advocate for its advancement.

The Judge

Jacob Safford, Jr., whom my family would eventually call "The Judge," had a sense of purpose profoundly shaped by that education and his own beliefs.

Raised in a culture where slavery was regarded as a moral failure rather than a distant political issue, he came of age leaning in one direction. As he continued his education at Oberlin College, that framing sharpened into conviction. For a young man in his late teens, Oberlin offered not just education, but the knowledge that the world was taking sides. He trained in law and entered adulthood with the tools of a profession that placed him at the center of a rapidly changing nation.

To be anti-slavery in the 1850s was not a passive stance. It meant aligning oneself—socially, politically, and often professionally—against a powerful and deeply entrenched system. It meant accepting that the question of slavery would shape the nation's future and that neutrality would not be an option for long. For Jacob Safford, this was not simply an intellectual position formed in a classroom; it was how he understood justice, order, and the role of law.

"It is law," one student said, folding his arms, "and defended by many ministers as order."

"Then both law and ministry stand accused," Jacob replied. "A statute cannot make theft honorable merely because it is written. Nor can a pulpit wash cruelty clean."

The professor, an older man accustomed to youthful sureness, regarded him carefully.

"Strong words, Mr. Safford. Yet indignation alone frees no one. What would you have men do?"

Jacob answered without pause.

"First, refuse the lie that bondage is natural. Second, deny it respectability wherever it appears. Third, build places that do not bend before it—schools, courts, newspapers, and churches. If slavery depends upon silence, then speech is already resistance."

Another student shook his head. "Easy enough to say in Ohio. Harder said in Missouri or Kentucky."

"Then harder things must be done there," Jacob said.

The professor rested a hand on the lectern. "And if the nation will not yield?"

Jacob looked toward the frosted window before answering. "Then the nation will be made to choose what it truly worships—liberty in language, or liberty in fact."

No one spoke for a moment after that. Outside, the bell sounded across the yard. Inside, among young men preparing for professions and futures, the argument of the age had already entered the room.

This abolitionist background stood in clear contrast to the family his daughter would later marry into. His future in-laws, the McMeekins, had been shaped by different geographies, economic realities, and a social order in which slavery could exist as an accepted part of life and inherited custom. But history rarely leaves people neatly separated into opposing camps, and the crossings of lines—where sharply different moral worlds eventually met under one roof—remain among the most revealing turns in American history.

The generation that followed the most violent years in Kansas Territory entered a world where coexistence, compromise, and some measure of reconciliation became necessary. Whatever convictions their elders had carried, children and grandchildren were often left to build families and communities from the unsettled inheritance of those conflicts.

Oberlin College is where Jacob met Esther Coon, a fellow student, a trait common in Safford women. An interesting thread of family memory—unproven, but persistent— suggests that she herself may have had African American ancestry, possibly tracing back to either free Black or enslaved individuals. The historical record has not confirmed this, but if true, even in part, it would have placed their household in an even more intimate

relationship with the central conflict of the age. The question
of slavery inside the household was not a distant one; it
would have been bound up in the family itself and
impossible to ignore.

Esther Coon Safford

Whether that lineage will ever be proven, what is clear is
that Jacob entered adulthood with a worldview that left
little room for ambivalence. In a nation moving steadily
toward fracture, he stood on one side of a line that was

becoming harder to ignore—and eventually, impossible to avoid.

Esther and Jacob married on May 3, 1849, in Oberlin when they were both 21 years old. Within the year, Jacob had finished his studies, and they were living in Lorain County, Ohio, now engaged in the more practical effort of establishing a livelihood. The young family began a series of moves, first into Michigan, where their daughter Jennie was born in 1850.

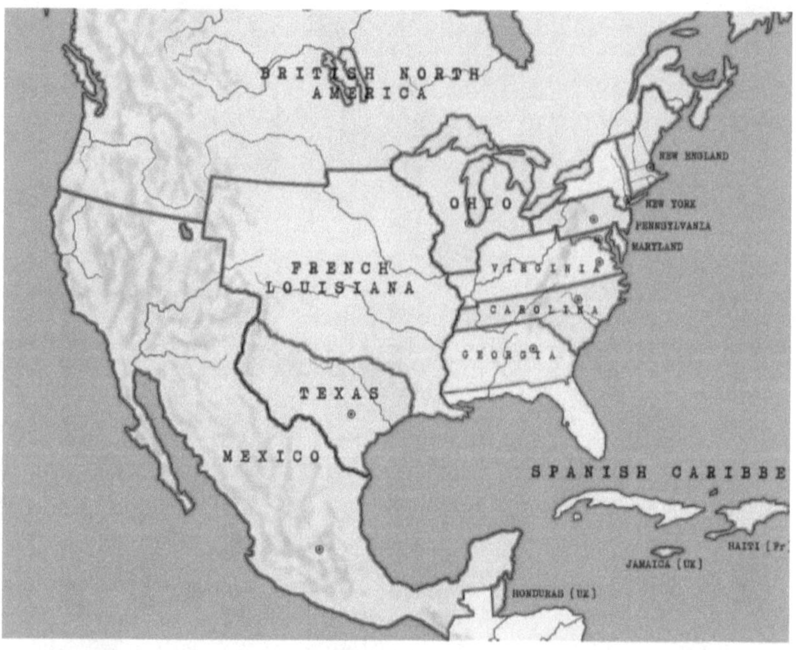

Map of United States in 1850

Within the decade, the Kansas Territory had become the focal point of a national conflict, drawing those who were willing to risk security for both opportunity and moral conviction. They decided to go west. Principle likely played its part, but the move was also driven by necessity. They were not heading toward the frontier in full strength. Jacob and Esther were sick.

Part 2 — Claiming Ground (1850s)

5

Billy Stealy: New York

WHEN BILLY STEALY WAS born sometime in the mid-1840s, Manhattan was overflowing. The city pulsed with daily arrivals from the other side of the Atlantic. Patrick Stealy and Mary Deegan had been among this human tide when they arrived in 1839.

Billy's first memories were of the constant activity and sounds of the urban metropolis: rumbling carts, waterfront workers advertising their services, and a symphony of foreign accents coalescing into an American tone. Childhood in such districts did not unfold gently. They learned early to be vigilant and to contribute where they could.

Then, as so often happened in immigrant communities, loss arrived swiftly. Within the span of roughly a year, Billy's parents were gone, the quiet calamities that defined working-class living in the mid-nineteenth century. In the weeks following his father's death, the household collapsed. Relatives and neighbors did what they could. Food was shared, temporary sleeping space was found, and promises were made in the hopeful language people use when they believe suffering will pass quickly.

But hardship lingered.

For Billy, the experience must have felt less like a single catastrophe and more like a slow unraveling. After his mother's death a year before, familiar routines disappeared.

Her voice, once a constant presence, fell silent. Adults spoke in lowered tones about practical matters he did not fully grasp. The sense of belonging that his parents had built in the immigrant neighborhood gave way. Then, almost suddenly, his father was gone as well.

In such circumstances, loss rarely came with a clear explanation. Billy would be formed by what followed. He understood what had been lost.

Illustration, Manhattan's Ward 14 c. 1855

Next came the aftermath. Thomas, his older brother, was old enough to become independent, but not secure enough to provide for his siblings. His sister, Mary, may have been taken in by a neighbor or the parish. But children like Billy, who were left without protection, became problems to be solved by institutions. There were few safety nets beyond the expanding network of charitable societies determined to impose order on what reformers described as urban chaos.

Billy was now one of the many children that Manhattan could not afford to keep. Somewhere between tenements and official care, between memory and bureaucratic preservation, his future narrowed into a question others would answer for him: what should be done with him? Survival required immediate decisions.

One morning, officials arrived without warning.

Billy may have first noticed them as strangers in the doorway — better dressed than most in the neighborhood, carrying papers that granted an air of authority. They spoke softly with the adults present, their voices calm and deliberate. This was not the first time they had come to such a building. It would not be the last.

He would not have been asked for his opinion. Decisions were presented as protection, opportunity, and moral guidance. Words meant to reassure. But beneath them lay a simple reality: the structures of family and community had reached their limits.

Someone gathered Billy's belongings. There was little to pack. A change of clothing, perhaps an object that was his mother's or father's — small enough to carry, significant enough to anchor memory. The walk to the waiting carriage was short.

Neighbors watched from doorways. Some offered blessings. Others avoided eye contact, unwilling to witness another quiet fracture in a neighborhood already marked by loss. Reformers believed they were rescuing children from environments of neglect. Residents understood that rescue often came at the price of separation. Billy climbed aboard because there was nowhere else to go.

For thousands of immigrant children in mid-nineteenth-century New York, this transition was less an event than a gradual surrender — a reduction of options until the state or charitable societies stepped in.

As he pulled away, the streets that had formed the landscape of his earliest years receded into distance. The displacement ahead — toward institutional care and the island facilities rising in the East River — was undefined. What he could sense, even then, was that this movement marked more than a change of address. It marked a change in who would shape his future. From that moment forward, he would not be guided by kinship, but by systems: by administrators, crusaders, and eventually by the vast national forces that would carry him west and into war.

Randalls Island

Randalls Island lay just beyond the restless movement of Manhattan. Reached by ferry or boat, it housed a growing complex of almshouses, hospitals, and orphanages intended to contain the human consequences of urban expansion. Activists spoke of moral rescue and discipline. Administrators spoke of capacity. Children learned to speak very little, if at all.

At the children's home, names were written down. Ages estimated. Backgrounds compressed into brief notations that could never capture the texture of what had been lost. In large dormitories lined with narrow beds, individuality softened into routine. Days were measured in bells and instructions. Meals came at fixed hours, and work and lessons filled the spaces between.

Illustration, Randalls Island c 1855

Billy woke each morning to the alarm and watched as the dormitory filled with children. The rhythm was predictable, almost soothing. The routine provided a kind of relief: a predictable program, with food arriving on schedule as proper, balanced meals. Then, by evening, erasure set in. Billy realized he had not heard his own name spoken all day. He was now a number, and his history, a notation. He learned not to keep anything that might be taken. Friendships formed quickly and dissolved just as fast as children were transferred, apprenticed, or sent away. Attachment was a risk few could afford.

Outside the windows, the East River ran with steady indifference. Ships passed carrying goods, immigrants, soldiers, and news of a nation reshaping itself. The skyline continued to climb. Opportunity, wealth, determination — all the forces that defined American expansion — were still visible but distant, like a promise addressed to someone else.

Billy watched. He listened and learned. Institutional life required adaptability, and silent observation often mattered more than strength.

By the late 1850s, a new idea was taking root: send the children west. This was how nineteenth-century America solved problems. Children would be sent to farms and rural townships that they believed could offer healthier moral and physical environments. To bureaucrats, this was progress. To the children, it was another departure.

The Orphan Train Movement

New York and other eastern cities were full of children like Billy — Irish, English, German, nameless mixtures of all three — the surplus population of a country growing faster than it understood itself. Epidemics, industrial accidents, injuries, and sheer exhaustion took parents early. Charitable activists worried about what they described as a growing class of "street children" — unsupervised, unemployed, and in their view at risk of becoming criminals or permanent dependents. These were boys and girls too young to work and too numerous to be easily cared for.

At the same time, the United States was expanding westward at extraordinary speed. Railroads pushed into territories that only a decade earlier had been Indigenous homelands or sparsely settled zones. New states like Illinois, Iowa, Kansas, and Missouri were being transformed into agricultural regions that demanded labor — steady, disciplined, and inexpensive labor. Farm families struggled not only against weather and markets, but against the simple reality that building a working household required many hands.

One solution came from the Children's Aid Society, founded in New York in 1853 by activist Charles Loring Brace. Brace and his colleagues believed that environment shaped character. If urban children could be removed from what they considered corrupting influences and placed in rural Protestant households, they might grow into productive citizens. Rural living could provide food, fresh air, and a sense of purpose that was difficult to achieve in city tenements. The effort was framed as moral rescue as much as economic relief. Churches often encouraged participation, framing it as both charity and civic duty, while others saw it only as a practical advantage. The result was that beginning in the 1850s, trains were organized to transport groups of orphaned children westward.

These relocations would later be called the Orphan Train Movement, one of the largest child relocation programs in American history. Between roughly 1854 and the early twentieth century, an estimated 200,000 children were sent from eastern cities to communities across the Midwest and Great Plains.[1]

The trains became a moving transition between desperation and hope. At scheduled stops, locals would gather to inspect the children, as farmers might examine livestock at market. Some looked for strength or obedience. Others, perhaps, for companionship or the chance to reshape a life. Some genuinely wished to offer care and opportunity.

Children could contribute labor almost immediately — tending animals, assisting with planting and harvest, performing household chores. Formal adoption laws were still in development, and these placements often functioned as apprenticeships or informal foster arrangements. Outcomes varied widely. Some children were deeply integrated into their new families. Others experienced neglect, exploitation, or repeated relocation.

Geographically, the trains traveled through expanding rail corridors. The local papers announced arrival dates, and residents gathered at depots or church halls where children were presented for selection. Decisions were made quickly, based on impressions formed in a matter of minutes.

For boys like Billy Stealy, the experience represented both rupture and possibility. The farm families who stood waiting on rural platforms were themselves participants in this larger transformation — settlers building livelihoods in unfamiliar landscapes, negotiating their own struggles for stability even as they became agents of change in the lives of displaced children.

The meeting of these worlds, at once compassionate and transactional, would define the next chapter for Billy.

❖

THE NEWS OF LEAVING the island washed over Billy. He didn't feel excitement so much as the familiar anxiety of starting over. Another chance at belonging.

The morning of departure started unceremoniously. Children were woken earlier than usual, told to gather their things, and form lines in the yard. Instructions were followed, and names were called. Decisions had been made elsewhere. One by one, children stepped forward to stand before a table where administrators observed them with professional attention. Physical condition was assessed. Notes written in neat handwriting that reduced complex lives to brief descriptions: strong, reliable, suitable.

He stood among them, trying to read the faces of the adults who briskly performed the preparations. When his turn came, he stood straight, answered questions without decoration, and avoided drawing attention to any emotion he could not safely express.

Across the room, some children were being gathered into groups. Billy waited for the decision. When his name was finally listed among those scheduled to leave, the moment passed without acknowledgment. A mark on a page. The conveyor belt of improvement pushed forward, steady and unyielding. He had been evaluated, selected, and assigned a path he did not design.

A ferry waited at the dock. Its paint was worn by years of service. The air smelled of river water and coal smoke. As they boarded, the island that Billy knew so well suddenly looked small. It had been a setting for his grief, his adjustment, and his gradual grasp of survival. Now even that temporary certainty was being taken away.

The boat pushed off with a low shudder. Then the distance began to grow. Randalls Island slipped behind them, its buildings shrinking into pale shapes against the gray winter sky. Ahead, Manhattan rose in layered lines of brick and chimney smoke, alive with the energy that had first drawn his parents across the ocean.

Billy went toward the rail. He did not know whether he was being sent toward opportunity or toward another form of loss. Around him, younger children clutched each other or stared silently at the water. Some had been told they were going to new families or that they would have work. The words blurred together, difficult to trust.

Ice drifted in slow, grinding fragments, and barges passed heavy with cargo. A steamer's whistle cut through the cold air, reminding everyone aboard that commerce and progress were larger than any individual.

For Billy, the crossing marked another quiet severing. Whatever ties he held to the streets of his earliest memory — the crowded rooms, the voices of kin, the warmth of his family — were dissolving into distance. Ahead lay a future described only in generalities: farms, responsibility, a chance to become useful.

He watched the shoreline change as the ferry angled toward the mainland. Somewhere beyond the docks, beyond the rail yards and gathering crowds, waited the train that would carry him forward. He could not yet imagine what that meant. Over the water, his familiar room in Ward 14 receded into memory. Ahead lay only the west.

❖

STEAM FROM THE ENGINE drifted towards the train platform in slow white currents. To Billy, it seemed like a living thing: enormous, restless, and cold to the tiny figures

being guided toward its open doors. There was no crowd
gathered to see them off. Only organizers moving efficiently,
checking lists, counting heads, ensuring that the day's
arrangements unfolded according to plan. They stepped
forward in uneven lines, each carrying whatever remnants
of life had not yet been taken from them.

Illustration, Train Station c 1855

He climbed the narrow metal steps and entered a railcar.
Wooden benches lined the walls, and windows were
streaked with grime. He found a seat with some older boys,
who were already hardened in ways no child should be.

They clutched paper tags pinned to their coats. Others had nothing that marked them except the watchful attention of the adults who had assembled them. A few younger children whimpered in the subdued, exhausted way that followed too many changes in too little time.

No one told them how long they would travel. Inside the car, stillness settled. Some boys spoke in low voices about farms they had never seen.

"Do they really give you a horse?" one asked.

"My brother says they need boys for milking," another answered, though he had no brother at all.

"I'd rather have a bed," a smaller child muttered, drawing a few thin laughs.

Some wondered whether there would be apples in the summer, if the people out west were kind, or if they would be kept together or split apart the moment they arrived. One boy insisted he would run back to New York if anyone tried to whip him. No one replied to that. Others stared straight ahead, conserving what little emotional strength they had left.

The whistle sounded abruptly. A single, rising note, and then the train lurched forward with the inevitability of a choice already made. Billy watched the platform through the window, trying to fix details in his mind — the outline of buildings, the curve of track disappearing into the distance. As New York grew farther away, Billy crossed into uncharted territory. Ahead lay Illinois. War. Marriage. A brief life that would ripple forward through a lineage he would never see.

History often remembers generals, presidents, and great voyages in sweeping numbers. Opportunity. Manifest Destiny. This expansion would be called progress. But the story of the American nineteenth century was also written in moments like this: a boy on a train, sent west by forces he did not control, toward a future he would help create. Billy could not know which version of his future was waiting.

Outside the windows, the eastern cities unraveled into stretches of raw countryside, factories giving way to fields, brick giving way to sky. Prairie, timber, and rivers that did not yet carry the names they would later hold. Somewhere out there was Illinois and the people who would take him in. Somewhere out there was the path that would lead him, still barely grown, into the uniform of a Union regiment.

The wheels hammered a steady rhythm beneath him.

---

[1] Scheuerman, Dan (November–December 2007). "Lost Children: Riders on the Orphan Train". Humanities.

6

Billy Stealy: Monmouth, Illinois

THE TRAIN SLOWED. THE whistle sounded sharply over the open ground, a lonely sound in the vastness. At once, the children surged toward the windows, crowding shoulder to shoulder, and pressing their faces against the glass to catch the first glimpse of what lay outside. Small hands smeared the panes.

"Look there—wagons!" one boy cried, pointing at a pair of teams moving beside the tracks.

"Horses too!" another shouted.

A girl near the back whispered, "Is that the town?" as she stared at a scattering of wooden buildings, grain elevators, and storefronts rising from the dust. Someone spotted women in bonnets gathered near the platform.

One boy announced with certainty, "They've come to see us."

Beyond the station lay a world unlike the brick streets and narrow alleys they had known: open sky without end, wind bending the grass, fences stretching toward the horizon, and bright sunlight falling hard on raw lumber and packed earth. Men in broad hats stood waiting beside wagons. Farmers leaned on rails. Curious children clung to their mothers' skirts.

The matron rose sharply from her seat and barked for them to sit back down, her voice cutting through the excitement like a switch through tall grass.

"Back now. Sit proper."

Reluctantly, the children pulled away, though many kept twisting in their seats for one last look.

Billy stayed where he was. He sat stiffly, hands clenched in his lap, his gaze fixed not on the window but on the scuffed toes of his shoes. He had no wish to see what awaited him. Whatever was beyond the glass was not home, and no amount of grassland sunshine could make it so.

The station itself, when the train finally slowed beside it, was little more than a low wooden platform and a narrow clapboard depot weathered gray by sun and dust. A small crowd had gathered with curiosity. They studied the children with narrowed eyes, calculating their usefulness. Someone opened the railcar door.

Cold air rushed in, stinging the lungs. One by one, the children were told to step down. Billy felt the ground beneath his shoes — softer than Manhattan's streets, rough, carrying the smell of farm animals and cut hay.

Illinois did not look like the stories. There were no shining farms or welcoming banners. There was just a landscape so vast that it spread in every direction with an emptiness he had never imagined. The tall tawny grass bending beneath the wind like waves on a silent sea. Above it arched an immense blue sky, so wide and unbroken that it felt as if the world were exposed, with nowhere to hide. A water tower stood nearby, leaning slightly, and beyond it, hitching posts, and a few buildings marked the edge of a town that looked unfinished, as though it had only just been planted there.

He stood with the children in a loose line, waiting to be chosen. That was the worst part.

The farmers approached first, studying the boys with practical interest. Questions were asked about age, strength, and experience with farm work. Could he read? Was he strong? Had he worked before? Some children were turned slightly so the light fell across their faces. Others were told to walk a few steps or lift an object as proof of capability. Women stood just behind, their expressions harder to read. A few whispered together. Some avoided looking directly at the children, as though acknowledging too much humanity might complicate whatever outcome they had come to make. Billy stood still. Around him, choices unfolded quickly.

A boy scarcely older than Billy was led away by a man who seemed satisfied with what he saw. A younger child smiled openly as a woman took his hand and guided him toward their waiting wagon. Plans were spoken about meals, about a home, about becoming part of a family — words that sounded both hopeful and final.

Billy re-boarded the train, where several spaces in the row were now empty. Relief and dread mingled in equal measure. Being chosen meant a kind of certainty. Remaining meant continuing into more unknown towns and unknown prospects. At each stop, lives diverged. Roads closed, and new ones would open. He would step onto another platform soon enough, and his future would likely be decided before sunset.

The train pulled away.

Advertisement for Orphan Train, c 1910

Monmouth, Illinois

THE TRAINS BY NOW familiar movement shifted from a steady pace to the harsh squeal of brakes engaging and wheels grinding against the rails as it slowed. Inside the car, conversations faded. Everyone knew what was coming next.

Billy straightened without realizing he had moved. Through the window, he saw the station, this one smaller than the last one. The organizers acted quickly once the train stopped. Children were helped down from the car and arranged in loose rows. Hats were adjusted. Bundles straightened. The scene by now was familiar.

The crowd had begun to thin as children were led away in different directions, their futures agreed upon in exchanges that lasted only minutes. Billy stayed in line, trying to steady the restless energy gathering in his chest.

Then he noticed the couple. They did not approach immediately. Instead, they stood slightly apart, watching in a way that suggested deliberation rather than idle curiosity. The man was between thirty-five and fifty, though the range hardly matters — the years had compressed into a single texture of weathered skin. Broad across the forehead, creased at the outer corners of the eyes from squinting into flat midwestern light, his cheeks and nose darkened to a permanent reddish-brown that stops precisely at the hatline.

He is built for endurance rather than brute strength — not slight, not imposing, but solid in the way that a fence post is solid, set deep and resistant to lateral pressure. His palms calloused in specific places that map the tools he favors — the handle of a scythe, the grip of a plow — and there is a permanent darkness worked into the creases of his fingers that soap does not entirely reach. He keeps them clean enough.

He is not a dirty man. His clothes are sturdy and mostly mended. Wool trousers in the colder months, linen or cotton in summer, held up by suspenders because a belt is one more thing to buy. His boots are his single significant expense, and he treats them accordingly, greasing them in the fall, watching the soles through winter, resoling them when he can, and living with the consequences when he cannot. He owns a coat that was good once.

He does not say a great deal about his opinions — about soil drainage, about the reliability of the Conestoga wagon versus the farm wagon, about his neighbor to the east whose fence line wanders in a way that suggests either carelessness or intention — but he keeps them in good order and produces them only when the occasion seems to warrant it. His wife knows what he thinks. Strangers generally don't try. Now his eyes moved with practical focus from one boy to the next, measuring what Billy could not quite name.

The woman's gaze was different. She seemed to be studying not just bodies but expressions — searching for signs of temperament, resilience, perhaps even trustworthiness. Billy had encountered adults like this before: teachers on the island, administrators in selection rooms. People who believed they could understand a child's future by observing him closely enough.

A question was asked, and Billy stepped forward when prompted, answering simply. His voice sounded unfamiliar to him — older than he felt, shaped by years of learning when speech helped and when silence protected. The matron spoke on his behalf, offering assurances about his reliability and willingness to work. Billy listened stoically. Assurances offered in such settings were more for adults than for children.

The man nodded once. The woman hesitated. In that hesitation, Billy felt the uncertainty that defined his life. Selection meant movement. Movement meant survival. But each beginning required surrendering whatever attachments he had begun to form.

Finally, the decision was made. He was told to gather his things. There was no assurance that this choice would lead to true belonging or if it would be just another temporary arrangement. As he walked toward the waiting cart beside the couple, Billy felt the familiar mixture of relief and apprehension settle into him.

He climbed into the back of the wagon beside a sack of grain and a coil of rope, the boards rough beneath his hands. As they drove away from the platform, he did not turn around. Looking back had never changed anything before.

❖

MARGARET MACKEY HAD NOT planned to stand on a train platform that morning. The day had presented its usual demands. Animals needed tending, and bread required baking. The late-season wind had begun to dry the fields, offering both opportunity and worry. Farm work did not allow for idle curiosity. Every hour spent away from physical labor had to justify itself.

But the printed notice had lingered in her thoughts. Children from the East were coming. Boys who could help. Boys who needed homes. The minister had spoken about it the previous Sunday, describing the effort as both practical and righteous. A chance to do good while strengthening one's household. In a region where labor shortages could determine whether crops were planted or lost, the idea held undeniable appeal.

Her husband viewed it more directly. The land did not forgive inattention. A fence left unmended through one wet spring could mean a season's worth of livestock wandering into a neighbor's corn. Timber left uncleared was ground left unplanted, and ground left unplanted meant they would go hungry. A farm did not run itself, and it did not run on good intentions. It ran on hands.

Hired labor existed but cost money that moved through a middling farmer's household like water through cupped palms — present briefly, then gone. The arithmetic was simple and unforgiving: more workers meant more acres worked meant more harvest meant survival edging toward something that might, in a good year, resemble progress. An extra pair of hands, even small ones, even a child's, could tip that calculation. Families knew this. They took children in accordingly — orphans, the children of dead neighbors, boys and girls whose own families had too many mouths and not enough table. Whether this was charity or pragmatism depended largely on who was telling the story, and when.

So the Mackeys rode into town together. The depot was already crowded with farmers standing in tight clusters, discussing weather and yields while casting glances toward the track. Women lingered at a distance, weighing considerations that were not easily spoken aloud. Bringing a stranger into one's home altered its delicate balance. Kindness could not erase the risks.

When the train finally appeared, conversation faded. They watched as children were directed down from the cars — thin figures in ill-fitting clothing, carrying modest bundles that suggested lives repeatedly reduced to essentials.

Margaret felt her chest tighten. These were not the sturdy farm boys she had imagined. They were quieter. Watchful. Marked by experiences she could only partially understand. She wondered what they had been told about the experiment or about the families waiting to claim them.

Her husband stepped forward first. Practical questions mattered. Age. Strength. Experience, if any. The reformer responded with rehearsed assurances. Good boys, he said. Eager to prove themselves. Grateful for the opportunity. She studied the line. Some boys tried too hard to appear confident. Others seemed defeated. Then she saw one who stood very still, observing everything without drawing attention to himself. His clothing was worn but carefully arranged. His gaze turned from adult to adult with a concentration that suggested experience beyond his years.

"That one," her husband murmured. Margaret did not answer immediately. She was thinking about winter. About illness. About whether kindness offered once could be sustained through seasons when survival itself was at risk. Taking a child meant more than adding labor. It meant accepting responsibility for a child already shaped by loss.

The whistle sounded again. They would have to decide quickly.

<hr>

THE WAGON WHEELS STARTED turning before Billy had fully settled into the seat.

The man, Mr. Mackey, coaxed the horses away from the station with a soft click, his movements quick with the confidence of frequent trips into town. The train's whistle sounded once more, then dissolved into the distance.

For several minutes, no one spoke. Billy sat with his satchel resting against his knees, aware of every minor movement. The boards beneath him vibrated with the rhythm of travel. The leather harness creaked. Hooves struck packed earth in steady measure. The surroundings were in stark contrast to what he had known. In New York, distance had been measured in blocks and crowded intersections. Here it stretched outward in unyielding lines. Fields lay in various stages of cultivation — some turned dark and ready, others stubborn with roots and stones. Clusters of trees rose like islands in a wide sea of sky. The openness unsettled him. There was nowhere to disappear.

Margaret Mackey sat opposite him. She watched the road at first, then the boy, then the road again. Billy sensed the same careful weighing he had seen earlier.

"You've worked on a farm before?" she asked at last.

Billy shook his head. The admission felt risky, but pretending to possess knowledge he did not have could prove worse.

"We'll teach you," Mackey said matter-of-factly from the front seat without turning around. They traveled in this manner for miles. The sun shifted westward, flattening the colors of the landscape into muted gold and brown. Billy noticed details he had missed at first: the smell of cut hay, the distant lowing of cattle, the way the wind blew like a living presence.

When the farmhouse finally appeared — low, wind-beaten and surrounded by fields still waiting to be tamed — the sun had begun to sink.

That night, Billy lay awake listening to sounds he had never heard before. Cows shifting in darkness. Wind against loose panels. Voices in the other room discussing him as though he were already part of the household inventory.

Midwest Farm Scene, c 1855

He knew then that his future would be a test of endurance.

IN THE MACKEY HOUSEHOLD, Billy occupied a space that was neither that of a son nor that of a servant. He lived as a hired boy would have, his usefulness earning his place at the table. He ate with the family, shared their routines, and absorbed their expectations. At night, he likely slept in a loft above the barn or in a narrow side room so he could hear the early stirrings of the farm before dawn. His days were measured less by clocks than by weather, livestock, and the steady demands of farm life that could not be ignored.

Spring was the hardest. As the frost retreated, the labor began in earnest. Fields had to be broken open with a plow and team, the iron blade turning soil that had lain stiff all winter. Corn was planted by hand in single, disciplined rows. Fences damaged by snow or wandering stock were mended post by post. Manure was hauled and spread to coax another season's yield from exhausted ground. Livestock required constant tending. At thirteen, he handled the horses, driving them across uneven furrows, guiding the plow while the animals strained forward.

Summer tested endurance. Haying demanded speed and strength, the cut grass gathered and stacked before sudden storms could ruin it. Water was hauled in heavy barrels that left deep ruts in the yard. Grain was shocked into upright bundles beneath an unrelenting sun. Animals needed feeding, milking, and watchful care. The toil stretched from sunrise to sunset. Shoes wore thin or were set aside altogether. It was not uncommon for Billy to go barefoot in the fields, his soles toughened through exposure.

With autumn came harvest and preparation — corn husking, woodcutting, hauling loads to town — but it was winter that altered the rhythm most profoundly. Farm labor slowed as snow sealed the ground and daylight shortened.

What the farm offered was not comfort, but expectation. Food appeared when tasks were done, and shelter was given as long as usefulness lasted. No one asked where he had come from. No one needed to. The past became irrelevant.

In these months, Billy also attended school, a detail preserved in the census but carrying far greater significance than the simple notation suggests. Instruction in reading, writing, and arithmetic offered him what many rural children never received: the tools to move beyond pure physical labor. Literacy widened his future. It would allow him to interpret contracts, follow orders, correspond, and eventually navigate the adult world with a degree of independence that would shape the course of his adulthood long after his years on the Mackey farm had ended.

❖

MONMOUTH IN THE LATE 1850s was a town in transition. Streets existed, storefronts were going up, and the drays came and went — but its edges were still unresolved, its center not quite settled. Older eastern cities had the confidence of proven fact. Monmouth, like most rural outposts, had only intention.

Blacksmiths, merchants, and tradesmen clustered near the center of town, their buildings flush against one another. They stood behind counters or in doorways, watching everything, tracking movement. They understood that stability was not given here; it had to be built, transaction by transaction. After Main Street, the buildings simply stopped, giving way to open fields. The boundary between town and not-town was a matter of a few steps.

Billy knew every foot of it. A boy moving through a place like Monmouth in those years was a kind of antenna — absorbing what the adults around him said and what they didn't say too. He ran errands and watched. He loitered at the edges of conversations that were held in a low, serious register. Information moved fast in a town that size. A broadsheet, a church pew, a comment made at sufficient volume outside the dry goods store — news didn't need a telegraph when gossip traveled on foot.

The people talking in the square had not been born here. He could hear it in the vowels — still carrying Ohio, Pennsylvania, New York, not yet worn flat by the prairie.

They had come west with tools and trunks and something harder to pack: a set of assumptions about how a place ought to work. How many lots should be platted, how debts should be honored, how a town should present itself to the world.

Street Scene, Monmouth, Illinois, c 1858

Billy would have watched them carefully. Not out of judgment, but recognition.

Monmouth also kept its moral life on display. On Sundays, labor stopped, streets quieted, and people moved toward the churches in their best attire, not finery necessarily, but clean and decent. Religion and reform were not separate currents but moved together, and the sermons reflected it. A preacher was not likely to confine himself to scripture alone. The country was coming apart along a single seam, and everyone in the pew knew it. Slavery was not abstract; it was openly debated. While Illinois was a free state, the Mississippi River was not far, and on the other side of it, the world was organized differently, slave-holding and determined to advance. Billy grew up inside that noise.

Monmouth College also gave the town an intellectual register that went beyond its structures — the sense that what a man believed about the country's direction was of some consequence. Kansas was talked about in the way people converse about something already on fire. They called it Bleeding Kansas, and even a boy who didn't understand the full weight of the phrase could absorb what surrounded it: that something was being decided, and those decisions would matter here.

The town did not erupt into violence — not yet. But it held the tension the way the prairie holds weather: invisibly, over distance, building without announcement until the day it doesn't. Monmouth was still in transition. So was Billy. And in the space between those two processes—unfinished place, unfinished boy—the larger country was beginning to take shape in ways neither of them could control.

7

Ben McMeekin: Kansas Territory

Kansas Territory, 1854

THEY ROSE BEFORE DAWN, not because they wanted to—but because they had to. The heat would come fast once the sun cleared the trees, and the horses did not move the loaded schooner easily in it. So the effort of leaving began in darkness, in that narrow band of time when the world was still cool and undecided. A lantern burned low in the yard.

Mary Jane was awake. She had been for hours. The last things were gathered not in haste, but in deliberate focus—items checked and rechecked because once the wagon rolled, there would be no turning back for what had been forgotten. Inside, the children were still asleep.

H.D. stepped in, pausing for a moment as his eyes adjusted. The room looked different, stripped down and emptied of its contents. What remained was only what they could not take or had chosen to leave. One child at a time was lifted from the bed without fully waking them. Carried out into the cool air, wrapped in blankets against the morning chill. Gently placed among the goods packed the night before—nestled between sacks of flour, folded bedding, and crates tied down with rope.

There was a practiced efficiency to it. They stirred, but did not wake.

This was not improvised. They had been preparing for weeks, maybe longer. It was early spring, and the decision, once made, had turned quickly into logistics. What to take and what to leave. What could survive the road. Tools had been loaded first—axes, iron, the things that would matter most once they arrived. Then food, then what comforts could be justified. A plow, if space allowed, or at least the components to assemble one later. Barrels for flour, salt pork, and seed. Bedding. A few pieces of furniture, if there was room. A Bible and documents. Everything had been argued over in advance and measured against distance.

The Conestoga wagon was more like a sturdy farm cart. It was not elegant or designed for comfort, but built to carry. Chickens were tied into crates, and a milk cow was driven alongside. He checked the harness by feel in the dim light. Leather straps. Buckles. The animals shifted, already sensing movement. Quiet, hushed words when there were any were exchanged. There was nothing much left to say.

They left before the light came. The wagon resisted at first, contents shifting, wheels sinking into the ground before surrendering to it. Then the motion took hold, the creaking settling into rhythm, and Kentucky began to fall away behind them. The fields they had worked. The home they had built.

Dawn came, revealing the route as it went. Grooves deep enough to grab a wheel. Tree lines that closed in and then opened. They were not following a single road so much as a network of unwritten paths — down through Kentucky toward the Ohio River crossings, then into southern Illinois or along the Mississippi corridor, depending on which way circumstance pushed them. Thousands had traveled it. That did not make the trek any easier.

The distance was not great, just a few hundred miles. A wagon averaged 10 to 15 miles a day under good conditions. Rain cut that in half. Mud could stop it entirely. In a decade or two, it would take just a matter of hours by rail. But they were not traveling by rail, and a few hundred miles at the speed of an oxen and a loaded wagon could take a season. They kept moving.

Illustration, Covered Wagon Migration

Kentucky's settled farms gave way to stretches where houses were more spread out. The air warmed quickly once the sun rose, and by midmorning the advantage of their early start was already being spent. The children woke, confused at first—then aware of movement, of change. Mary Jane settled them as best she could, managing discomfort without complaint. There was no room for that either.

By midday, the heat pressed down. Grasshoppers snapped through the open expanses as the timber thinned and finally disappeared altogether, leaving them engulfed in a vast sweep of primeval grass—rosinweed, bull's-eye, and redroot stretching to the horizon. Along the winding creeks, narrow bands of sandbar willow cut green ribbons through the prairie.

H.D. hunted game along the way: pronghorn antelope grazing the short grass that, at the slightest hint of danger, exploded across the plains like arrows released from a bow. Prairie dogs popped from their cratered towns and barked in nervous curiosity at passing riders. Their burrows were dangerous places to probe too carelessly, often shared with rattlesnakes coiled in the cool dirt below or burrowing owls blinking from the shadows.

They would stop briefly—water the animals, stretch, eat a simple meal of bread or dried meat—but never long enough to lose the rhythm of the day. Distance was everything now. Every mile gained early reduced what remained.

By afternoon, the heat grew heavier. Dust lifted and hung in the air. Wheels sank deeper in soft stretches. Conversation, when it came, was minimal—functional. The effort of moving replaced the habit of talking. Then, toward evening, they would make camp.

Not elaborate or permanent. Just enough. The wagon would be drawn off the road, and a small fire would be built if wood was available. Food prepared quickly. The children laid down again, this time more aware, more restless. The animals tended, and the sky was a blanket above them. And then sleep—because the next day would begin the same way. Before light, before heat. Before doubt could take hold.

When they arrived in Kansas, the next phase of work began. Their first structure was not a house. It was a simple shelter, and the process of building it was direct and physical. Trees were felled with axes, cut low, trunks left where they dropped or dragged aside with effort. Limbs stripped. Brush piled and burned when dry.

Then came the first building. A log cabin, because it could be built with what stood around them. Logs notched at the ends, stacked one over the other. No sawmill required—just skill and time. Gaps filled with chinking—mud, clay, sometimes mixed with straw to hold it. A roof framed with poles, covered with split shingles if they had time, or rough boards, or even bark in the earliest stage.

The floor might be packed earth at first. Later, puncheon logs were split and flattened. It was a single room. There was a fireplace built from stone or clay at one end, because heat and cooking were not optional. Smoke billowed out imperfectly until the chimney drew correctly. Light came from a door, perhaps a window cut later. This could be done in days, if urgency demanded it. Weeks, if done more carefully. They would have slept inside it before it was finished.

Everything that followed came after that first enclosure. Ground was next cleared not just for space, but for planting. That meant more trees, more burning. Crops planted between them in the first seasons—corn often first, because it would grow where other things struggled. Water had to be secured—a spring, a creek, or a dug well. Fences were built to keep what little livestock they had from wandering.

Each improvement layered on the last, none of it optional. There was no illusion about comfort. H.D.'s role in Kentucky—farmer, trader, landholder—did not accompany them. The homestead required daily, visible proof.

Mary Jane's responsibilities included managing children with no immediate neighbor to turn to if danger erupted suddenly, and making order inside a structure that had begun as raw timber and earth. She had to preserve what little food they had. Stretch it. There was no separation between domesticity and survival. Danger with a young son underfoot was everywhere. Ben was only four.

They had not come west because they had nowhere else to go. They came because Kansas offered a position that could still be taken and a future that was not yet assigned.

❖

Hayden "H.D." McMeekin

H.D. WAS BORN IN 1822 in Shelbyville, Kentucky, into a family accustomed to movement and reinvention. By mid-century, he was no longer part of the settled East. His parents, Charles McMakin and Elizabeth Duncan, engaged in trade rather than subsistence farming, operating a dry goods business. This was a world where supplies, credit, and exchange mattered more than property alone. At the age of twelve, he began working in the dry goods store owned by his parents, learning the rhythms of trade long before he reached adulthood. For the next decade, he remained behind the counter, measuring cloth, tallying accounts, unloading freight, and dealing with the constant stream of travelers, farmers, and townspeople who passed through the store. Those years trained him not only in merchandising, but in the practical social skills that frontier life demanded: negotiation, persuasion, patience, and the ability to read men quickly.

By 1844, restless for opportunities beyond his hometown, he left the family business and met and married Mary Jane Lawrence, part of another family with deep colonial roots— a parallel line moving westward through the same channels of opportunity. The young couple moved to Munfordsville, Kentucky, where H.D. spent another four years working in tobacco shipping and merchandising. The tobacco trade exposed him to the expanding commercial networks pushing westward through the Ohio Valley and into the Mississippi River economy. Flatboats, wagon routes, and river commerce connected towns like Munfordsville to a rapidly changing national market, and ambitious young men sensed that fortunes would increasingly be made farther west.

It was likely during these years that H.D. became involved in the Mexican–American War. Family recollections and later frontier stories suggest he served in some capacity during the conflict in 1845–46, though surviving records remain uncertain. The experience would have placed him among thousands of young Americans drawn into the vast southwestern campaigns that opened new territories and accelerated the national obsession with western expansion. In later years, stories from the war reportedly became part of his identity—tales retold around campfires, trading posts, hotel lobbies, and saloons, where veterans mixed memory with exaggeration until fact and legend blurred together.

In 1850, he was still in Kentucky, where his name appears on the slave schedule for Oldham County. It is a brief list, but a definitive one. He, like his father and grandfather, was participating in the system that underpinned much of the southern and border-state economy, and that would soon define the political struggle in Kansas. Later that year, he moved. Not directly into Kansas, but to its edge—to Weston, Missouri, a river settlement functioning as a staging ground for westward movement. Though he would not again be recorded as the owner of enslaved people, he would instead commit himself to the defense of slavery publicly, politically, and with substantial force.

In Weston, he opened a store and entered more fully into the trade networks, pushing toward the frontier. He established trading relationships with the Potawatomi and operated a post near what would become Rossville, Kansas—positioning himself not as a settler tied to a fixed address, but as a man working the space between established communities and emerging ones.

Fur companies had established trading posts across Missouri and Kansas, functioning not only as depots for commerce but also as fortified outposts in an often-disputed countryside. Dealers, trappers, and hunting parties had passed through the region for decades, drawn by its rich animal populations and its strategic position between eastern markets and the western plains. The land teemed with wildlife. Vast herds of buffalo dominated the steppe, joined by deer, elk, and antelope, while wolves and foxes roamed freely. Along the rivers and streams, beaver, otter, mink, and muskrat meant the waterways were especially valuable to the fur trade.

Independent fur suppliers and Indigenous people participated too, bringing in pelts to exchange for goods such as tobacco, alcohol, cloth, and weapons—transactions that frequently disrupted the missionaries' efforts to reshape Natives through conversion and farming. For a time, these resources were central to the economy, but by the middle of the century, the richest trapping grounds had been depleted, and the center of the fur trade had pushed farther west into the Rocky Mountains.

Missouri was established, slaveholding, and economically tied to southern systems. To the west stretched acres that were not fully claimed in the American sense—inhabited, traveled, and challenged well before any formal territorial lines were drawn. Kansas held no established towns, no stable legal framework, and no assurance about what the region would become. What existed instead was a shifting borderland—part trade route, part rumor, and part political fault line. Maps existed, but they did not yet govern anything. Men traversed into it without permission because there was no authority to grant it. Pioneers passed through on their way further west to Oregon or California, carrying families who did not intend to stay. Military patrols appeared and disappeared. Goods passed through, and information passed faster. It was not a location. It was a corridor.

———————————❖———————————

Spring, 1856 — Kansas Territory / Pawnee Land

BEN WAS IN THE field that morning, close enough to see the cabin, but far enough to feel the pull of being six — half working, half wandering. The morning had settled into its rhythm: simple chores, dirt under his nails, and the slow movement of time that marked living on the borderlands.

Then something shifted. Movement near the cabin. Not his father, or a neighbor — there were hardly any of those yet. Shapes where there should have been none. Several tall figures standing on the front step.

He froze. For a moment, he did nothing at all, his mind trying to catch up with what his eyes were telling him. Then it landed all at once: Sallie. She was inside, four years old, and alone.

He dropped what he was holding and ran. The ground blurred beneath him, uneven and hard. His breath came fast, sharp, the kind that burns in the chest. He did not call out. Instinct told him not to — not yet, not until he knew. The cabin grew larger with every stride; the rough boards, the rough-cut doorway, the place that meant safety, now occupied by something unknown.

He slowed only when he reached the door, his hand brushing the frame as he pulled himself to a stop. The air inside was cooler, dimmer. For a split second, he hesitated — then stepped in.

And everything he expected was wrong.

Sallie sat near the table, exactly where she should not have been if anything was amiss — upright, calm, talking. Always talking.

Across from her, two Pawnee men sat near the stove, crouching easily in the small space, as if the cabin belonged to them as much as to anyone. They wore heavy buffalo robes thrown over deerskin leggings, their moccasins still damp with prairie frost. Silver armbands caught the firelight at their wrists, and each carried at his belt a knife in a decorated leather sheath and tobacco pouches that were beaded in faded blue and red. Their presence filled the room, but not with violence. They had come in without asking. They would leave the same way.

One of them held a strip of salted beef, chewing slowly. The other reached toward the table, selecting an item with the casual confidence of someone who did not recognize the boundary between taking and being given.

Sallie was speaking to them as if they were neighbors, with the fearless ease of someone too young to understand danger.

"That piece is too salty," she informed the first man, pointing at his food. "Mama keeps the better meat higher up."

She studied the second man's coat. "Why are your buttons different?" Without waiting for an answer, she continued.

"We got a calf outside. It kicks. Ben says he can catch it, but he can't." She turned and called toward the doorway,

"Right, Ben?"

Then back again: "Do you have horses? Have you got any children? My doll's arm came off."

The men did not answer. One chewed. The other glanced at her briefly, then back to the table.

Illustration, Ben and Pawnee in their cabin

Ben stood in the doorway, breathing hard, waiting for a raised voice, a sudden movement, anything that would confirm the danger he had imagined on the run. Instead, the room held only the scrape of teeth on meat, the rattle of the kettle lid, and Sallie's bright, unbroken chatter filling the silence.

Nothing did. One of the men glanced at him, not startled, not threatened. Just aware. His gaze held for a moment, then shifted back to the room, to the food, to the small girl who continued her quiet chatter as if this were an ordinary visit.

Ben did not move. He watched as they finished what they had taken, and then, just as easily, gave something back. They set down several tiny quail. An exchange without negotiation. They rose without hurry. Without apology or explanation.

As they stepped past him into the light, Ben turned slightly, his body tight, ready in a way he had no words for. But they did not look back. Within a few steps, they were part of the land again—moving away from the cabin, over ground that did not belong to the McMeekins any more than it belonged to them.

The quiet returned just as quickly as it had been broken. Inside, Sallie looked up at him.

"They were nice," she said.

Ben said nothing.

<hr>

ACCOUNTS FROM THE PERIOD describe H.D. as one of the more successful figures connected to the Indian trade, participating with Native groups that linked him to people who did not share the same assumptions, but were connected through exchange. H.D's early trading post meant that interaction between settlers and Native groups was regular, informal, and shaped as much by proximity as by necessity. His success depended on relationships: trust, barter, hospitality, and the ability to navigate cultural boundaries in a volatile borderland where federal authority remained thin. One account recalled visits from local inhabitants in simple terms: they casually came and went from his cabin, and left gifts of small game, signaling a familiarity that blurred the boundaries between domestic and commercial space. It's a memory his children would recall decades later.

<hr>

"The Indians were very friendly, and they brought my brother [Ben] and me presents of quail and birds they caught in cages they made. Indeed, they were too friendly, for they would walk into the kitchen and pick up anything they fancied."
- Sallie McMeekin

<hr>

Those years were marked not only by opportunity, but by hardship and epidemics. Around 1849–1850, cholera swept repeatedly through frontier settlements, military posts, and river towns across the Missouri Valley. Uniontown and nearby regions were deeply affected. Emigrant caravans carried the disease westward along the overland trails, while crowded river traffic spread it rapidly between settlements. Death could come within hours. Entire camps were sometimes abandoned. Travelers buried victims hastily beside trails and riverbanks before moving on.

Within a few years, however, the ground beneath him was shifting. The same federal system that issued licenses and regulated trade was now advancing a different agenda: Manifest Destiny. The republic, Washington argued, was meant to spread westward, carrying its systems and people to the Pacific.

The vision felt grand and inevitable. Trails stretched farther onto the plains, and the discovery of gold drew fortune-seekers to California. But the creed carried a harder truth beneath its shining surface. The liberty so often praised was not intended for everyone. Enslavement still scarred the nation for much of the era, and Native peoples stood directly in the path of the future Americans imagined for themselves. For expansion to proceed, tribes would have to surrender land, autonomy, and ways of life that had endured for generations. Most refused.

Those living on indigenous homelands experienced it as an invasion. The same movement that built towns, enriched speculators, and linked oceans also brought removals, broken treaties, military campaigns, and the steady compression of Native homelands. Progress and dispossession advanced together, each driving the other west. It was policy in action: treaties negotiated under pressure, land cessions extracted, and Native nations pushed—again and again—further west.

The Potawatomi had already experienced that displacement. Originally from the Great Lakes region, they were forced west in the 1830s through a series of removals tied to federal Indian policy. As white settlement advanced, the space between Native nations and incoming settlers did not hold—it collapsed. And those positioned in that space would not remain neutral within it.

Illustration, Trading Post c 1848

Fur trapping was one of the harsher and lonelier occupations, drawing young, rugged individuals willing to trade comfort for danger and profit. In late fall, they disappeared into the river country, following creek beds and wooded bottoms where animals were plentiful. There, they built rough winter camps—half-buried dugouts cut into the earth, their log fronts chinked with mud, roofs covered in sod or brush to keep out the wind. Smoke curled from crude chimneys into the frozen air, often the only sign of human activity for miles.

Their days started before dawn in bitter cold. Wrapped in buffalo robes or heavy wool coats stiff with frost, they silently set trap lines beside icy streams and marshes, where beaver, otter, muskrat, raccoon, and bobcat wandered through mud or snow. On the open grasslands, they laid heavier traps for wolves and coyotes, animals prized for their pelts but dangerous when cornered. Each catch had to be skinned carefully, the hides scraped clean, stretched taut on wooden frames, and cured by firelight inside cabins thick with the smell of smoke, damp fur, and animal grease.

Camp was physically punishing and never secure. Food came partly from what was carried in, but often depended on what they could hunt—deer, wild turkey, rabbit, or whatever game could be found. Nights were spent mending gear, drying boots stiff with frozen river water, and listening for sounds beyond the firelight: prowling wolves, sudden storms, or the approach of strangers. Spring thaw brought swollen rivers and the end of the trapping season, when the men packed their bundled pelts onto horses or wagons and went back to their settlements. If the season had been good, they might carry back several hundred dollars' worth of furs—a small fortune at the time, earned through months of isolation, exposure, and relentless labor.

When H.D. McMeekin was trading on the Kansas rivers, these newcomers were living on ground that had only recently been assigned to them—and would not remain theirs for long. What appeared, for a moment, as coexistence and exchange was, in fact, a closing window.

In the early 1850s, as pressure mounted to open Kansas, merchants and traders tested routes westward. Shallow-draft boats ferried supplies inland—food, tools, hardware— linking the Missouri River system to the developing interior. H.D. was part of that early movement. Contemporary accounts place him traveling those routes, noting that the Kansas River was no harder to navigate than the Missouri. It sounds like a practical detail, but it shows that he was present within the machinery of early westward expansion.

H.D. pushed farther west, arriving at Fort Leavenworth, then one of the great gateways to the frontier. Established along the Missouri River, the fort stood at the crossroads of military movement, emigrant migration, Indian diplomacy, and overland commerce. In 1855, H.D. took a preemption claim in the Salt Creek Valley near Fort Leavenworth, one of the first and most competitive outposts in Kansas. Federal law had granted lots that could be occupied, improved, and then secured. There, he built what was described as the "fourth house" in the town, continuing a pattern that would define his movements: arriving early, building quickly, and positioning himself at the edge of what came next.

Kansas in the 1850s demanded endurance at every level. Beyond the few scattered towns, settlers experienced profound isolation with no railroads, few passable roads, and almost no reliable communication. A simple trip for mail or provisions could take days by ox team, and neighbors were often miles apart. Streams were unbridged,

trails poorly marked, and winter storms could erase all
sense of direction, turning ordinary travel into real danger.

The white population numbered around 1,200 people
then—roughly half were soldiers stationed at forts, while
the rest were associated with missions or trading posts.

These settlements, raised from grasslands, were little
more than surveyed claims and a few structures, and were
always competing for dominance. Daily existence was
stripped to necessity. Most families lived in rough cabins
with homemade furniture, surviving on simple food like
cornbread, bacon, and whatever game or wild fruit could be
found. Illness spread easily, and when sickness struck,
entire families might suffer alone without a doctor or nearby
help. Women bore the hardest burden, often spending
months managing multiple children, illness, food shortages,
and fear in near-total solitude.

But H.D. was never a homesteader; he understood that
the first profits on the frontier were not to be made in
farming. Farming required stability—clear title, predictable
markets, and neighbors who intended to remain. None of
that existed yet. Real security would come from trade—in
supplying the movement, not settling it, and from
positioning himself where the country had to pass.

Supply outposts, transport, lodging—these were the
businesses that formed before permanence. He was among
an early wave who were watchers, brokers, and
opportunists—men who knew the ground would change
and intended to change with it. In that way, he did not farm
the frontier: he worked its timing.

As Leavenworth began to rise, property values followed. H.D. sold his claim at a profit and shifted focus. While he maintained his trading post connections, he also assumed more formal roles, serving as a deputy U.S. marshal and later as the deputy sheriff of Leavenworth County during the border conflicts. But in those earliest years, before towns solidified and authority fully took hold, H.D. operated within that transitional space—where proximity and insecurity defined daily life.

❖

KANSAS REMAINED FORMALLY UNDER Indigenous control until 1854, when Congress formally organized it as a United States territory. That year signaled the beginning of large-scale white settlement and a profound and painful upheaval. Native nations that had previously been driven into Kansas under federal commitments and told that the land would be theirs "as long as the grass shall grow," were forced to move once again, now farther south into what would later become Oklahoma. Their removal cleared the way for white development, opening Kansas to a wave of occupation even as it shattered earlier guarantees offered in treaty after treaty.

To most Americans, Kansas was still little more than a distant name on a map—a vast stretch of fields in the remote western desert, known chiefly as Indian country. But those who had covered it on overland trails to California often spoke of it in strikingly different terms. Travelers arrived from the east with reports of fertile soil, open fields, and remarkable natural beauty. Some who had earlier seen

Kansas only in passing later came back to claim territory there themselves.

What came next was not a peaceful opening of the territory, but the start of one of the most turbulent chapters in American expansion. In the twelve years that followed, Kansas turned into a countryside of violence, political upheaval, and bitter division. The struggles that erupted were the direct consequence of the nation's deepening fracture over slavery, as North and South turned Kansas into the proving ground for a battle that would soon engulf the entire country. What had seemed a distant, vast prairie suddenly stood at the center of America's most explosive political struggle.

Present in North America since the colonial era, slavery had become ever more entrenched in the South, where the invention of the cotton gin transformed cotton into a highly profitable crop and meant enslaved labor would become central to the plantation economy. In the North, where industrialization was reshaping society and slavery had never taken deep economic root, opposition to its expansion grew stronger with each passing decade.

As the nation expanded westward, every new territory raised the same volatile question: would slavery be allowed to spread? Southern leaders sought to preserve and enlarge the institution, seeing it as essential to their economy and political power, while many Northerners resisted its extension into an area they believed should remain free. To preserve a fragile balance in Congress, lawmakers tried to admit states in pairs—one slave, one free—but each compromise only postponed the reckoning.

The Missouri Compromise of 1820 was one such attempt at containment. It admitted Missouri as a slave state but prohibited slavery in the remainder of the Louisiana Purchase north of Missouri's southern boundary. By that definition, Kansas was designated free soil. Yet it settled nothing permanently. As years passed, Northern writers, churches, and abolitionist societies condemned slavery with increasing urgency, while clandestine networks helped enslaved people flee northward to freedom. In Congress, debates over slavery grew more bitter and combative. By the middle of the nineteenth century, the conflict had moved from political disagreement to national rupture, and most Americans felt that war was no longer avoidable.

The crisis erupted with the Kansas-Nebraska Act, which left the decision on slavery up to the settlers themselves — a concept called "popular sovereignty." In theory, the question would be settled by vote. In practice, it became something else: people did not arrive in Kansas solely to build homes or farms. They came to secure outcomes. Pro-slavery and free-state settlers alike rushed into the territory, determined to secure its future.

The land broke open.

Pro-slavery Missourians crossed the border into Kansas to stake claims on large tracts, in some cases before the removal of Native peoples had even been completed. Some came intending to establish genuine homesteads, building cabins and settling as the law required. But most had no intention of becoming permanent residents. Instead, they marked claims symbolically—by notching trees, posting notices, or laying out rails in the rough shape of a cabin—

then returned to Missouri, ready to come back only when elections approached, or armed action was needed. Their purpose was not residency but political control. Kansas would be physically claimed and organized by intimidation and force, if necessary.

From the North, anti-slavery settlers and abolitionists arrived with equal purpose, intent on preventing it. However, the path into Kansas for these pioneers was far more difficult. Unlike the Missourians, who could cross the border in a matter of hours, free-state settlers often came from hundreds of miles away, from New England, Ohio, or other northern states. Their journeys required far greater expense, planning, and sacrifice. Families had to leave established communities behind and travel extensive distances into a territory that offered few of the structures needed for civilization.

Kansas still had almost none of the foundations that made subsistence bearable: there were few formal communities, almost no schools or churches, little reliable shelter, and scarcely any newspapers or organized civic prospects. To persuade northern families to uproot themselves for such ambiguity was no easy task. Yet despite these disadvantages, many came, driven by a conviction that Kansas had become more than just farmland—it had become the ground on which the future of slavery in America would be decided.

H.D. moved into that space at the right moment, shifting fluidly through the early territorial economy. When settlements were laid out—sometimes more on conjecture than certainty—he was there. He participated in the first

layer of development: commerce before permanence.
Buildings went up quickly. So did expectations.

IN THE SPRING OF 1854 the Missouri ran high and brown with snowmelt, carrying whole trees in its current and the smell of distant thaw. Boats battled slowly against it, paddle wheels beating a steady violence into the water. On their decks stood those who believed they were traveling toward potential. Toward property ownership and the right to begin again.

They could not yet see what they were entering. The Kansas shore lay low and deceptive — a long green embankment rising from mud. Grass bent in the wind, and cottonwoods leaned toward the current as if listening. Somewhere inland, survey stakes had been driven into soil by men who did not own the land. Maps had been drawn in distant cities. Town names chosen. Futures priced and advertised. All before most Americans could even have found Kansas on parchment.

The law had arrived only in theory. What existed in truth was motion. Wagons creaked westward across the bottomlands carrying stoves, seed corn, rifles, whiskey barrels, and printing presses. Young men with soft hands and older men who had already failed somewhere else. Speculators who believed that history could be hurried if enough money pushed it forward. Preachers who believed the same thing for different reasons.

Some had come to make Kansas free.

Others had come to make it slave.

Most had come simply to make themselves. They built towns the way card players built hands: convinced that confidence alone might shape reality. There were names of places that might not survive the season and names of men who would not survive the week. The papers in the East called it an experiment.

Among those stepping onto the bank that year was H.D. McMeekin. He had come, like thousands more, because the nation had opened a door and promised that what lay beyond it could be claimed. Land. Trade. Influence. A future that might belong to whoever reached for it first. Where the business of building America would be conducted in sawdust-floored hotels and on muddy riverbanks. The decisions made by the people in these raw settlements — who traded, who voted, who hosted, who survived — would ripple outward for decades. Through war, statehood, and through families who would carry the memory of this violent beginning long after the prairie itself had been fenced and parceled and renamed.

Spring wind blew over the plains with a restless persistence, flattening the pasture in slow waves that seemed almost tidal. Wagons stood scattered near the riverbank where the first arrivals had camped, their wheels sunk deep in mud softened by thaw. Smoke rose from cook fires. A saw rasped somewhere beyond sight. They spoke loudly as if volume alone might transform belief into reality.

They began marking the streets before they had finished clearing the meadow. Someone had decided where the town would be. There was no vote. No ceremony. Just a few stakes driven into the earth were enough to convert open ground into surveyed lots, each measured with confidence that bordered solely on faith. Maps had been drawn in advance — rectangles and street names imagined in distant offices where speculation cost nothing but ink. Here, reality required labor.

"Main Street runs straight through here," one man declared, tapping a stake with his boot.

"Straight through grass and buffalo wallows," another muttered, wiping sweat from his neck.

A third unrolled a paper already curling in the wind.

"Bank lot there. Hotel here. Depot just east once the railroad comes."

"When the railroad comes," someone repeated, drawing a few dry laughs.

"Laugh now," the first man said. "In five years, you'll wish you'd bought on this corner."

Nearby, men lifted timbers, dug post holes, and hauled stone from carts. Hammers rang, and more dirt rose with every shovel turn. On paper, it already existed. On the prairie, it still had to be built.

The plot belonged to H.D. McMeekin. He watched as the first building took shape, little more than a frame at this stage. Rough timber had been hauled from upriver and fitted together with urgent resolve. H.D. had purchased the claim from a French Indian named Louis Vieux for $500. The transaction, however, involved no clean deed or survey. What H.D. acquired was older and less clear—an agreement recognized by those who had lived and traded there before American law arrived. Under federal law, such transactions often lacked formal standing, yet possession and use carried their own legitimacy.

The seller, Louis Vieux, was a French-Indian (Métis) trader and a significant figure in the history of the Potawatomi and Kansa (Kaw) tribes due to his Potawatomi heritage. He operated along the trade networks of the Kansas River. Vieux's ferry and later bridge over the Kansas River, known as Vieux's Crossing, played a crucial role in facilitating westward expansion and commerce on the Oregon Trail. They were between worlds, conducting trade via river routes, building posts, and establishing relationships with Native communities and with American officials alike. They held influence, but not always legal authority.

Whether Vieux possessed the right to sell the parcel was, even then, unclear. But H.D. was not buying certainty. He was buying position. And position—along a river, near a crossing, in the path of movement—was what towns were built on. Around him, settlers argued about frontage and property lines, about whether the ferry landing would remain stable enough to support trade. The river itself offered no guarantees. It shifted course when it pleased, disregarding human intentions.

Opportunity demanded speed. Lots were sold before boundaries were fully understood. Money changed hands in pockets and under wagon covers. Whiskey circulated freely, boosting optimism. Some newcomers spoke openly of fortunes waiting just beyond the skyline. Others kept their intentions private, measuring risk in silence.

A sawmill appeared beside a bend in the river. Then a blacksmith shop. Two lodges followed within sight of one another, each certain it would outlast the other. A general store, its shelves sparsely stocked but arranged with care. Billiard tables were hauled across hundreds of miles of plains so that men might practice civilization while improvising it. At night, lanterns glowed through the grass like a temporary constellation. Gunfire sometimes followed. Violence was never far away.

Rumors traveled the same routes as freight and livestock. Missourians had crossed the border again, someone said. A printing press destroyed. The argument over slavery — distant to some, urgent to others — infused even mundane transactions with tension. Deals decided in daylight might require defense after dark. H.D. understood the stakes.

He had come to claim his place in the machinery of growth that defined the American moment. Towns like this offered possibilities unavailable in older regions where hierarchies were fixed. Here, influence could be earned through initiative and a willingness to invest labor and reputation in surroundings that might yet justify such faith.

By morning, the prairie would look different. More stakes. More wagons. More trust layered over doubt. They were building towns faster than history could record them. Some would endure while others would vanish so completely that future generations might struggle to believe they had ever existed at all.

Then came the rumors. Surveyors had been seen upriver. A chain crew passed through at dawn, measuring distances no one else could yet interpret. They gathered in taverns to compare notes, tracing possible routes across crude maps stained by coffee and tobacco. Every conversation ended with the same uneasy conclusion: nothing would matter more than where the railroad chose to go. In Kansas, destiny arrived on paper before it arrived in track.

Investors in distant cities studied reports about river depth, soil stability, and projected freight volumes. Local boosters sent letters thick with enthusiasm, promising population growth that existed mostly in imagination. New businesses opened in anticipation of customers who had not yet even left.

Indianola believed it had a future.

Its river position suggested a natural advantage. Warehouses stood near the landing, and wagons rolled regularly through muddy streets that residents insisted would soon be graded and widened. Property lots changed hands at prices unthinkable only a season earlier. To doubt the town's prospects felt like betrayal.

Then the announcement finally came. A notice posted in Topeka confirmed what some had begun to fear: the rail line would pass three miles away. Engineers cited practical considerations: terrain, cost, and projected efficiency. Their reasoning was sound, and their decision was final.

Initially, they refused to believe it. Surely the route could still be altered. Petitions were drafted. Delegations organized. Arguments rehearsed about fairness, about investment already made, about the injustice of condemning an entire community through a single calculation. Yet railroads did not negotiate with hope. They followed capital and momentum.

Indianola, Kansas, 1854

Indianola changed almost immediately. Merchants postponed shipments, and prospective settlers continued west rather than stopping. Buildings that had symbolized permanence were short-lived. The same wagons that had once delivered lumber now took furniture away. Opportunity, it seemed, possessed a geography of its own.

While Indianola faded, Topeka rose in corresponding measure. Track met open ground, and streets appeared. Warehouses multiplied. Inns expanded to accommodate the steady influx of travelers seeking connection to the wider nation. Political influence consolidated around those who controlled access to infrastructure.

H.D. adapted. His experience had taught him that attachment must remain conditional. The future belonged not to those who loved a place most fiercely, but to those willing to follow movement wherever it led. He shifted his operations toward Topeka, investing labor and reputation in a city whose prospects aligned with the steel lines advancing over the grasslands.

In later years, people would describe Indianola's decline with a mixture of nostalgia and resignation.

"It was killed by the railroad," they said. The truth was more complicated. For families building their lives in Kansas, the lesson was unmistakable. The nation's future would not be determined solely by elections or ideals. It would be engineered — measured in miles of iron, calculated in freight tonnage, secured through the quiet authority of infrastructure that rewarded some communities while bypassing others entirely.

Once again, movement dictated survival. And those who understood how to read its direction would help define what America became.

The Teft House / McMeekin Hotel, Topeka

FOR H.D., TOPEKA OFFERED opportunity on a different scale. By the time it began to resemble a permanent town, power no longer announced itself through rifles or claims. It gathered in rooms. Hotels stood at the center of this new order. They were among the earliest buildings constructed with intention — spaces designed not merely to shelter travelers but to organize movement itself.

Topeka was becoming the gathering point for those intent on shaping its future. H.D. knew that hospitality could be a form of authority. A man who controlled beds, meals, and meeting space also controlled information. H.D. could hear plans before they reached the papers and observe rivalries forming over late-night whiskey. He could watch reputations rise and fall across polished tabletops worn smooth by negotiation. To run a hotel in Topeka at that time was to stand at the intersection of commerce and power.

With the expansion of railroads, traffic had to land somewhere. In Topeka, it landed at the Teft House, also known more informally as the McMeekin Hotel, after H.D.'s purchase in 1858. Travelers arrived carrying portfolios instead of rifles, their aspirations expressed through contracts, legislative proposals, and carefully cultivated alliances.

H.D.'s earliest experience as a hotel proprietor had started with The Planters House in Leavenworth. From its onset, it was not a neutral place. Conceived in 1855, its purpose was political as much as commercial: the hotel was controlled by southern men and conducted on "southern principles"—no abolitionists were admitted.

Early Day Leavenworth Kansas by Alexander Gardner.

Public Domain

123

The founders, freighter W. H. Russell, H. P. "Hog"
Johnson, and Amos Reese, were tied to the Missouri River
trade and to the slaveholding interests just across the
border, likely associates of H.D.'s from his Missouri days.
They built quickly and on a scale meant to dominate. The
result was a four-story brick hotel, widely described as the
finest in the West outside of St. Louis. Its dining room
stretched more than 100 feet, seating 200 guests at a time.
The furnishings were imported and expensive, the
silverware of New York manufacture, the total cost reaching
a staggering $50,000.

The investment only made sense in context. Leavenworth
was the commercial extension of Platte County, Missouri—a
slaveholding region flush with agricultural wealth. Like
every frontier hotel, it functioned as a nerve center—part
boarding house, part political hall, part marketplace of
rumor and allegiance. Farmers, traders, and freighters
moved constantly between Weston and the Kansas Territory,
bringing with them not only goods but expectations about
how that territory should be shaped. The Planters House
became their outpost: a place where business, politics, and
identity converged under one roof.

But by 1857, the economics of exclusivity collapsed
under the pressure of a changing city. The hotel was sold to
Len T. Smith and Jep Rice, who abandoned the ban on
abolitionists and opened the doors to anyone who could pay
and behave. The shift was less ideological than practical.
Leavenworth, formally a controlled extension of Missouri,
was becoming divided.

Inside the Planters House, that contest played out in real time. The proprietors adopted a strategy as improvisational as the territory itself. In the basement barroom, two bartenders worked side by side—one pro-slavery, one abolitionist—each encouraging his own clientele, each absorbing the rhetoric that spilled across the counter. Arguments were tolerated. Threats were common. Only when violence crossed a line—when a knife struck wood or a pistol was drawn—did management intervene, sending the offender out the door regardless of allegiance.

Illustration, Leavenworth Planters Hotel, Public Domain

Around this time, H.D. shifted his interests to Indianola and then to Topeka, where the frontier phase of his life had given way to something more structured, more urban, and more profitable. After becoming proprietor of the Tefft House in Topeka—the leading hotel in the capital, it became known informally as the "McMeekin House." The Topeka papers listed its guests in columns of ink: "today's arrivals at McMeekins," as if it were the local depot or courthouse.

They recorded a steady stream of politicians, speculators, military officers, and territorial officials. The hotel welcomed merchants, drifters, and those moving west or returning east.

Inside, the rhythms were constant. Boots on wood floors. Trunks dragged in from wagons. Conversations drifted from supper tables into the late evening. People arrived there before they became anything else in Topeka. Some would stay. Some would leave. Some would return years later with different fortunes. Lawyers debated constitutional language in upstairs parlors while speculators tracked railroad expansions that would redraw economic geography yet again. City leaders cultivated support in dining rooms, where alliances were measured not only by votes but also by personal trust. Cowboys passing through shared intelligence from distant counties.

Teft House / McMeekin Hotel on Kansas Ave, 1868 Public Domain

Lobby conversations shaped perceptions of emerging leaders, and deals concluded over breakfast could determine the location of rail lines or the fate of legislative initiatives. H.D.'s position placed him inside this current. He was neither governor nor general. His authority derived instead from proximity. By later life, he wore a heavy patriarchal beard and spectacles that gave him the appearance of an aging frontiersman, part trader, part hotelkeeper, part unofficial host of the Kansas frontier.

The McMeekin Hotel was not separate from Topeka's growth—it was part of its foundation. The building itself was one of its earliest and most prominent establishments. It stood on Kansas Avenue, not grand by eastern standards, but substantial enough to signal longevity. The structure was wood-framed, two stories, with a broad front that faced the road—its porch worn by constant traffic, its doors rarely still for long. Dust from the street settled into the grain of the boards and never fully left.

Contemporary accounts described it as "first-class"—a distinction that mattered in a place where most buildings were still provisional. Visitors noted details that would have been expected in older eastern cities but were still rare in Kansas: Brussels carpeting in the second-floor rooms, with even the upper floors finished in a manner that suggested commitment. And most surprisingly, the building was equipped with gas lighting. That advantage alone set it apart. Where other establishments relied on candles or oil lamps, the McMeekin Hotel stayed evenly lit—its lobby and dining spaces active well into the evening, well after darkness settled over the street outside.

Tax lists show detailed inventories—beds, chairs, stoves, linens—evidence not just of a business, but of scale and purpose. This was not crude, temporary lodging. Inside, the air held a mixture that defined the era's commerce: tobacco smoke, wool coats damp from weather, leather, and the faint, ever-present trace of bourbon. The lobby was the center of it.

An extended counter ran along one side, scarred from years of use, behind which accounts were kept—room ledgers, payments, notes of who had arrived and who had not yet settled their bill. Keys hung in rows. Not all were accounted for at any given time.

Chairs were placed not for comfort, but for conversation. Men did not sit to rest. They sat to exchange information, and by late afternoon, the room filled. Travelers came in from the road—some from Missouri, or from deeper into the territory. Land agents, merchants, railroad men, and speculators passed through regularly. So did politicians, though they were not always identified as such. In Kansas in the 1850s, politics did not belong exclusively to formal chambers. It moved through rooms like this, delivered in segments, argued over in pieces, shaped in conversations that never appeared in official records. Just men leaning forward over bourbon, lowering their voices, pressing their points, and testing reactions. Deals were finalized with a handshake and their spoken word. A man might arrive unsure of his next move and leave with direction—what acreage to purchase, which partners to trust, and what risks to avoid. Someone else might come in confident and leave with that confidence undermined.

The dining room served the same function. Meals were served at dormitory-style tables, where strangers sat beside each other out of necessity. Formal introductions were brief.

What mattered was what each man knew and what he was willing to say. Plates were cleared, refilled, and cleared again as conversations stretched beyond the meal itself. News from the East arrived days or weeks late, outdated by the time it was heard, but still treated as immediate. Local developments mattered most: rumors of violence, shifts in territorial leadership, and the outcome of elections that were not always cleanly decided.

To an outsider, it was simply a busy hotel. To those who understood it, it was a clearinghouse, a stop where the future of cities and political alignment took shape one conversation at a time. And at the center of it was Hayden D. McMeekin— not simply keeping the books, but holding the room. He decided who was welcomed, who was tolerated, and who was gently encouraged to move on. He understood the shifting alliances—free-state men, pro-slavery men, and those who claimed neutrality but leaned one way or the other depending on circumstance.

It was all the same conversation: What would Kansas become? It usually started the same way: a group at a table, voices low, the conversation still indistinct from the others moving through the room. Plates half-cleared, and glasses not yet empty. Positions hardened, then softened when new reports entered the room. Then the mood shifted. A word held too long. A tone sharpened. Chairs angled closer.

Not land this time. Not railroads. Heavier.

A man from Missouri spoke first, leaning back slightly, as though the argument required distance to be made properly.

"You can't build a territory on sentiment," he said. "You build it on labor. Reliable labor."

Across from him, another man—newer to the region, less settled—answered too quickly. "Call it what it is."

A pause.

The Missouri man continued. "You think farms run themselves? You think this becomes a state without structure? We have a system that works. The South's proven it."

A third voice joined, now more deliberate. "At what cost?" That was when H.D. stepped in.

"The question isn't cost," he stated bluntly. "The question is what survives." The table shifted toward him.

He spoke the way you did when you had already chosen your position—not arguing to discover an answer, but to reinforce one.

"You don't hold a territory like this with theory," he continued. "You hold it with stability. With order. Labor is part of that. Whether you like the word or not."

The man across from him leaned forward.

"So you're saying Kansas becomes Missouri."

"I'm saying Kansas becomes something that lasts," H.D. replied. There was no apology in it.

Around them, the rest of the room continued as it always did—other conversations, other transactions, the movement of a space that did not stop for any single argument. But at this table, the lines were clear. Everyone understood what was being said. Not just preference or economics. Alignment. What mattered was not only what a man believed, but where he stood when it mattered. And H.D.

stood with those who believed the territory should allow slavery.

Voices rose. Others joined. Someone dismissed the entire argument as premature—"Let Washington decide it." Another rejected that outright. The word "legislature" surfaced, then lingered.

Outside, the wind drove dust down the street. Inside, the future of the territory was being molded: arguments reinforced, challenged, reshaped again. Some of those contentions would find their way into official rooms or votes. And soon H.D. would become a central player in the political struggle that defined the 1850s: Bleeding Kansas.

The Election of 1854

BEN REMEMBERED THE ELECTION, OR at least he held a memory of the activity of that day. Men had been stirring since before sunrise, voices carrying through the cool morning air as wagons rolled in and horses were tied off near the polling place. Strangers moved through the settlement with an urgency that children could feel, even if they did not understand it. Some wore pistols openly, standing in tight clusters, talking in low, heated tones.

By midday, the local square was crowded with tension. Men came and went with folded papers in their hands. Names were called out. Ben remembered his father telling him to stay close, then forgot it as the adults fixed their attention elsewhere. He did not know what was at stake. By the end of that day, the numbers told the story, and the scale of the fraud was not secret. At one polling location, only 20 of 604 voters were actual residents of Kansas Territory. At another, 35 residents were counted against 226 nonresidents. In Leavenworth, ballots outnumbered the population several times over. Everywhere throughout the territory, returns bore little resemblance to reality. What had been designed as an expression of popular will had been overtaken—systematically, decisively. And yet, it stood.

Illustration, Voting, Public Domain.

From that election, thirty-eight pro-slavery legislators took their seats. Thirty-eight men who were elected under impossible – and illegal – circumstances were given the authority to create laws in Kansas. And the group had one aim: to protect slavery. Among its "elected" members was H.D. McMeekin.

IN THE EARLY SPRING of 1855, the new legislature assembled. Governor Andrew Reeder had determined they would meet at Pawnee, which sat far to the west, removed from the Missouri border where the bulk of pro-slavery interference had originated. By placing the meeting there, Reeder was trying to put physical distance between the legislature and the forces that had shaped its election and give it a chance—however slim—for them to act with some independence. The men arrived, but they did not accept the terms.

Pawnee was inconvenient, they said. Isolated and lacking accommodations. But those were not the real objections. The problem was control. Pawnee was too far from Missouri and from their network of allies, reinforcements, and the intimidation forces that had secured its majority in the first place.

Before it had meaningfully begun its work, a bill was introduced to adjourn the session and relocate to the Shawnee Manual Labor School in Johnson County—just across the border from Missouri. The proposal did not linger. It was not debated as a logistical matter. It was understood for what it was: a repositioning of power.

The man who introduced it was H D. McMeekin.

The vote followed quickly; the measure passed, and with it, the center of government shifted east—out of the governor's reach and back toward the pro-slavery influence.

Reeder objected. He attempted to resist the move, arguing that the legislature had no authority to abandon the designated capital. It did not matter. The body simply left.

The move clarified that this was a legislative body intent on securing a position rather than governance, and willing to redefine the terms of authority to do it.

H.D.'s role there had not begun with the vote. He had previously aligned himself with the pro-slavery cause as a member of the Salt Creek Squatters' Association, one of several local organizations where land, politics, and allegiance were inseparable. In Kansas, claiming ground and claiming power were part of the same act. Because the legislature had been chosen through coercion, inflated numbers, and organized interference, and thereby did not possess the consent of those it governed, it would come to be enduringly referred to as the Bogus Legislature. And H.D. McMeekin was there at its beginning—representing a government that did not settle the question of slavery in Kansas, but ensured it would be fought.

Laws passed under its authority attempted to formalize slavery in the territory, impose harsh penalties on dissent, and consolidate control. Its first order was to simply import much of Missouri's slave code wholesale, transplanting into Kansas one of the harshest pro-slavery legal systems in the nation. Under these statutes, enslaved people were defined rigidly as property, and the rights of slaveholders were elevated above nearly every competing civil claim.

But property law alone was not enough. The legislature also sought to silence opposition itself. Printing or distributing abolitionist materials, or aiding any action that threatened slaveholders' rights, was also outlawed by the new legislation. Words were now treated as crimes. Those accused of aiding a slave revolt faced the possibility of death. Harboring escaped enslaved people or interfering with their capture brought severe penalties. The law was designed not merely to permit slavery, but to make resistance to slavery dangerous.

The assembly also purged dissenters. Lawyers, jurors, and officeholders were required in many cases to swear loyalty to laws protecting slavery, including federal fugitive slave statutes. This oath system functioned as a political weapon: Free-State settlers, though increasingly numerous, could be excluded from the machinery of government unless they submitted to a legal order most considered morally abhorrent and politically illegitimate.

What made these acts so explosive was not simply their defense of slavery, but their assault on the democratic process itself. The Bogus Legislature was not attempting persuasion or compromise; it was attempting legal domination.

For Kansans, even those not initially invested in the slavery question, this was the turning point. The process itself—the intimidation, the stuffed ballots, the visible manipulation—forced a reckoning. Neutrality was difficult to maintain when the basic mechanisms of governance had been overtaken so completely. The result was escalation. Free-State settlers formed their own rival government at Topeka.

By trying to secure slavery through the force of law, the Bogus Legislature achieved the opposite of stability. Its laws hardened divisions, destroyed faith in territorial governance, and transformed Kansas from a fractured frontier into a battlefield over the nation's future.

On March 19, the House of Representatives—now controlled by an Opposition coalition—appointed a three-man special committee to audit the territorial elections of 1854. What they found stripped away any remaining pretense. Out of the total votes cast, 1,729 were determined to be fraudulent, compared to just 1,114 that were legally cast. If the vote that fall had been limited to actual settlers, the committee concluded, the result would have been entirely different—a Free-State legislature, not the pro-slavery body that had taken power. It had been a coup.

But the finding did not settle the matter. On the ground in Kansas, the conflict was moving beyond reports and resolutions. On May 21, 1856, pro-slavery forces—many again from Missouri—entered Lawrence, the center of Free-State resistance. They burned the Free State Hotel, destroyed two antislavery newspaper offices, and looted homes and businesses. The event would be remembered as the Sacking of Lawrence, but it was less an isolated incident than a signal: the dispute over Kansas would not be contained within political bodies.

By August, it had become open warfare. Kansas was on fire. Pro-slavery men had been pouring into the territory for months. Free-State forces mobilized in response, and the violence that followed saw a steady stream of raids and reprisals, farms burned, and men shot in front of their families. The score was settled and then settled again.

In August, John Brown led a band of followers against a pro-slavery force at Osawatomie — some four hundred men against his handful. The fight was uneven, short, and brutal, and Brown lost it. He retreated, but Kansas kept burning. It would take two more months before the new territorial governor, John W. Geary, arrived and imposed something that resembled peace by the sheer force of federal authority and personal will. The guns went quieter, and the killing slowed. But Geary had only suppressed the conflict, not resolved it, and everyone on both sides understood the difference. Two governments still claimed Kansas. The question had not been answered. It had been postponed.

The postponement lasted years. Finally, in 1859, Kansas ratified a Free-State constitution and applied for admission to the Union. Southern senators blocked it. They understood the math: every free state that entered tipped the balance further against them, and they were not going to hand over Kansas without continuing to fight — not after everything that had already been spent there. The impasse held through 1859, through 1860, through the election of Abraham Lincoln in November of that year.

That was the tipping point. Southern senators walked out of Congress in the weeks following Lincoln's election, and the votes that had blocked Kansas simply disappeared. The chamber that had stonewalled admission for years found itself, suddenly, without enough opposition to sustain the fight, and Kansas was admitted to the Union on January 29, 1861. It entered as a free state — the thing it had been struggling to become for seven years, through fraud and murder and the long grinding failure of every institution that was supposed to have settled the matter peacefully. The larger war it had prefigured was eleven weeks away.

❖

WHAT CAME NEXT FOR H.D. McMeekin is a dramatic shift. After being part of the territory's earliest pro-slavery government, he leaves politics. The meetings, positioning, and legislative maneuvering give way to commerce—to the hotel, his enterprise, and the practical work of profiting from what would come next.

There are no records or letters left behind to explain why that shift occurred. Maybe the escalation—from disputed elections to intimidation, and then to open warfare—altered his calculation. Violence had become immediate, physical, and unpredictable. Participation had consequences that extended well beyond debate or lawmaking. It is also possible that nothing changed in his views at all, and he may just have determined that profits were to be found elsewhere. The reasons behind the change —whether from discomfort with the violence, practical self-interest, or some combination of both—are unknown. Did he recognize the failures of his earlier convictions? That hope may reflect my own desire for redemption more than anything the surviving record can prove.

H.D. would not be remembered merely for his size or appearance, but for the force of his personality. A newspaper tribute written after his death recalled how "that patriarchal beard waved welcome," and how guests arriving at his establishments felt immediately received into his orbit. The writer marveled that "everything that eats, sleeps and walks on two feet, from a politician to a Pawnee, passed through his hands." Even when his table was sparse, visitors left believing they had been generously fed. Another story claimed McMeekin once wrapped a freezing traveler in a fragment of fish net to keep him warm, an anecdote less important for its literal truth than for what it revealed about his reputation for rough frontier hospitality.

He had traded with Indians near Uniontown, witnessed the flood of migration along the California Road, operated hotels and trading houses across Kansas, and spent decades among soldiers, emigrants, speculators, trappers, politicians, and Native delegations moving through the borderlands of the West. By the time he walked Kansas Avenue in later years, beard flowing and spectacles glinting, he was less merely a businessman than a living relic of the territorial era itself.

Benjamin McMeekin

IT WAS INTO THIS world that Benjamin McMeekin came of age. Ben did not choose the frontier; he inherited it. He grew up in a world that had only recently been wilderness, where foundational structures—schools, churches, businesses— were still being built around him. As Ben approached adulthood, the early, chaotic phase of Kansas development had passed.

Topeka hardened into permanence. But freezing winters or bad harvests could still devastate communities, and economic shifts could undo years of effort. Families adjusted to conditions that were never entirely secure.

Ben lived in the shadow of what his father had established and worked within the framework H.D. had built. His life was less documented, less outwardly prominent—but no less tied to the conditions of those early enterprises. An upbringing built on movement, shaped by pressure, and sustained through adaptation had left a deeper instability that would surface again. When it did, it would not alter his life alone, but would define the childhood of his son.

What began in the eastern colonies, moved through Kentucky, and forged in the instability of Kansas, does not end there. It continues—west again.

8

Jennie Safford: Kansas Territory

Kansas Territory, 1858

IN 1858, JACOB SAFFORD and his wife, Esther, both had tuberculosis. They called it "consumption," the wasting disease, or 'the cough.' It was a condition that was as poorly understood as it was feared, and in the nineteenth century, it was one of the leading causes of death in the United States. The bacterial infection attacked the lungs, and victims rarely died quickly. Instead, they declined over months or years: persistent cough, fever, night sweats, and a gradual wasting away that gave the illness its name. It flourished in the very conditions industrialization was producing—dense cities, poor ventilation, and constant human contact. With no effective treatment before the late 1800s and no cure until the twentieth century, medicine could offer little beyond observation and advice.

What emerged was not treatment, but belief. Physicians and patients alike came to assume that climate could influence the course of the disease. Dry air, high elevation, and the open spaces of the western territories offered a chance, however unclear, of recovery. This idea drove thousands towards areas like Colorado, New Mexico, and parts of California, making them destinations for the sick. Men and women arrived chasing the possibility that distance, air, and environment might succeed where medicine could not.

Whether driven by hope or resignation, Jacob and Esther, both sick with the disease, prepared to move. The journey held risk. Kansas was volatile. It offered space, but little security. For a couple who were already in poor health, the decision to leave a comfortable home in the East and begin again on the frontier was not casual. It was a wager—on land, on climate, and on survival.

They traveled on a road that was little more than a trail, worn by oxen's hooves, schooner wheels, and weather into a series of grooves that grabbed at the axles and refused to let go. They moved at two miles an hour on a good stretch, less when the ground softened after rain, which it did often. They trekked for the better part of six weeks, moving through Indiana and Illinois before hitting the Missouri border, where the road narrowed, and the politics changed, and a man with a Kansas destination learned to be careful about who he told. The children rode when they could and walked when the wagon needed the weight off the wheels. Jacob and Esther walked most of the time. Everything they owned was in the dray behind them — furniture broken down to its component parts, tools wrapped in quilts, seed for a first planting that assumed they would arrive in time to plant it.

They started out in Lawrence, moved to Tecumseh, and eventually made their way to Topeka as it rose to become the state's political capital. This was how migration often happened—not in a single decisive leap, but in stages. Each move taking people a little farther from their point of origin, testing conditions, building resources, and preparing for the next step. His partnership with Esther reflected shared capacity; they arrived as a household equipped, as best they could be, for the uncertainties ahead. They did not arrive to ease.

The first winter proved exceedingly severe, and many settlers were not adequately protected against the sudden, intense cold. Most of the houses had been hastily constructed, one-room log cabins, with dirt floors and windows and doors of cotton cloth. Storms drifted into these cabins through countless chinks and cracks in the roofs and walls.

After surviving that bitter season, the Saffords decided to transport bricks from St. Louis to construct what was described as the first—or among the first—brick houses in Topeka. There were no railroads to carry such materials, which meant bricks were hauled overland, an effort reflecting both means and intention. It was a decision to build not for the moment, but for duration. Where most structures were still temporary, built quickly, and replaced just as fast, brick signaled the expectation of staying.

Then came the drought of 1859–1860, which pushed hardship into catastrophe. For sixteen months, rain scarcely fell. Wells dried, soil split open, and crops failed completely. With no reserves to fall back on, tens of thousands faced hunger. By the autumn of 1860, some 30,000 settlers had abandoned Kansas altogether, leaving behind claims they couldn't sustain. For those who remained, survival was precarious.

Despite the hardships, Jacob, Esther, and their daughters still found community and joy. Spelling bees, quilting gatherings, husking parties, and country dances brought people together across distances, often requiring miles of travel by wagon or horseback. These gatherings were essential social lifelines. Neighbors in Topeka visited freely and often, sharing chatter, labor, and companionship in a culture where hospitality was as much a necessity as a virtue—the pioneer saying that "the latch-string hung out at every door" reflected a world in which no visitor was turned away.

Hunting also provided both sustenance and excitement. Buffalo, antelope, deer, and wild turkey supplied meat for families and became part of the rhythm of seasonal survival. This abundance vanished with startling speed when the buffalo were driven toward extinction not by settlers hunting for food, but by industrial-scale slaughter for hides. Professional hunters killed them by the thousands, stripping skins for shipment east while leaving the carcasses to decay. Herds that had once stretched for miles disappeared in little more than a decade, erasing one of the defining features of the Great Plains.

Against this backdrop, Jacob Safford stepped into Kansas not as a visitor but as someone intending to contribute. It was a continuation of a pattern that stretched back to its beginning. Wherever the family went, they did not merely pass through. They built.

Kansas' legal and civic structures were only beginning to take shape, and Jacob did not remain on the margins but stepped directly into its core. When Kansas was admitted as a free state, the fight over slavery ended, but not everything was resolved.

The state constitution was a compromise, and like most, it gave with one hand while denying with the other. Some of its provisions were notable for the time. Married women were allowed to hold separate property—an important departure from the old assumption that a wife's legal identity disappeared into her husband's. Women were also permitted to vote in school elections, a narrow but genuine opening into public life.

But the larger gates remained closed. Full suffrage for women was denied. Black residents, whether free or formerly enslaved, were excluded from the vote. Native peoples were not recognized in the political community at all. Kansas had settled one great struggle, but order still rested on lines of exclusion that many would spend generations trying to break.

In 1859, Jacob Safford was elected a district judge for four years. He was guided by a steady conviction that slavery must not spread any farther west, that the Union must hold together, and that Kansas could only survive if governed by law rather than intimidation. He believed the state's future depended on building courts and governing bodies that people could trust. He then spent six years on the Kansas state supreme court, helping to establish the legal framework of a state when its identity was anything but secure. Where earlier lawmakers, including his future in-law, H.D. McMeekin, had used Kansas law as a weapon in the fight to impose slavery, Jacob's work was part of a different era: one of stabilizing courts, settling territorial disputes, defining civic authority, and giving permanence to a state whose identity had only recently emerged from conflict. His legacy was not written in fiery political decrees, but in the quieter effort of transforming a battleground territory into a functioning commonwealth.

❖

The Railroads

For decades before iron ever touched earth, the road was already there. Not in any formal sense — no graded surface, no surveyed line — but a path worn into the ground by repetition. Traders had been moving west since the 1820s, drawn across what mapmakers dismissed as the Great American Desert toward the markets of New Mexico. They came first with pack mules, then with drays capable of carrying larger loads across the 800-mile route.

Each spring, they gathered at Independence and Westport, Missouri, to organize into convoys. Schooners loaded with flour, bacon, coffee, sugar, rice, beans, and trade goods set out across the plains, drawn by mule or ox teams and sustained by buffalo and other game hunted along the way. They returned heavy with silver, hides, and whatever the plains had left of the men who crossed them. As traffic increased, so did tensions with Indigenous nations whose ground the trail covered, and trade routes that started as commercial ventures often ended up as scenes of conflict when mistrust and violence mounted on both sides.

Faint tracks deepened over time and passage. Hooves pressed them further, and seasons did the rest. Once they reached the open plains, the scenery changed dramatically.

Ahead lay hundreds of miles of uninterrupted ground—
more than six hundred miles without farms, people, or
civilization. Vegetation thinned, shelter was almost
nonexistent, and traders prepared accordingly, lashing
spare logs beneath their wagons for repairs since usable
wood could rarely be found along the route. Cottonwood
along a stream was an event worth noting. In dry months,
the dust hung in the air like a second sky. In wet ones, it
turned to mud so deep it swallowed wheels to the axle.
Campsites repeated year after year until the ground
remembered them. Graves marked the margins.

Map of Santa Fe Trail

By the 1840s, it had become a commercial artery, and
after the Mexican War, it pressed further to New Mexico and
California, now American territories. The route followed the
logic of survival: water, grade, distance, persistence. It was
the most efficient line across the plains because the people
who traveled it had no margin to be wrong.

When the engineers of the future Kansas railroad looked
at that worn path, they saw alignment. The terrain had

already been read and proven by men who could not afford mistakes. If pioneers had found the best route, iron should follow it. Claim the one that already existed. The railroad would advance mile by mile along a path that was already there, set down not by surveyors but by the simple pressure of people who needed to get somewhere and kept going until they did.

September 15, 1859 — Atchison, Kansas Territory

THE ROOM WAS TOO small. A dozen men crowded in early, coats brushed but not clean. They had come upriver by steamboat or overland along the same trails they were now proposing to replace. They knew each other—by business, by reputation, by necessity. In Kansas, there were no strangers among men trying to build something large.

A table had been set at the front, papers laid out in careful order. Windows stood open, but the air did not move. Voices filled the room, low at first, then rising with argument and calculation. Everyone understood the task.

For years, the Santa Fe Trail had carted the daily commerce of the region, but it was slow, limited and seasonal. A man could make money on it, but not control it. A railroad would change that. It meant speed and volume that no wagon train could match. It meant shifting from scattered trails and independent traders to fixed lines, controlled routes, and towns that rose or fell based on where iron was laid.

The question was no longer whether it would happen.

It was who would build it.

When the meeting came to order, the room tightened. Chairs scraped. Papers were gathered. Names were spoken, and written down. Jacob Safford was among them. These men, who would serve as directors, carried the authority of the territorial legislature and its charter: The Atchison and Topeka Railroad Company.

They spoke in practical terms—routes, capital, and the necessity of federal support. But beneath it ran an urgency: Kansas was still young and unstable. The men in that room were not simply organizing a company but selecting the future of a state and its broader national implications.

That day in 1859, there was hardly enough reason to justify the endeavor. Fewer than four thousand people lived along the proposed line. No cities. No markets, and no guarantee of return.

"We'll need county commitments first," one said.

"Without local bonds, the eastern money will never come," said another.

"Then we secure the right-of-way now," a third man replied. "Land grows dear the moment rails are certain."

Someone else tapped the proposed route.

"Bridges here, grading crews here, timber contracted before spring."

"And locomotives?" someone asked.

"When there is enough track to justify them."

They were not building a railroad so much as building the case for one—assembling figures, promises, charters, and confidence to carry steel across open country.

Outside, wagons still traveled on the old trail, wheels grinding through ruts carved by decades of use. Trade continued as it always had—slow, exposed, dependent on distance and weather. Inside, they were planning the end of that world.

When the meeting adjourned, the line had been drawn—first in ink, soon in iron.

❖

IN THE 1860 Topeka census, the Saffords appear in ink: Jacob, a young lawyer with a growing family, listed beside his wife, Esther, and their children. It is a simple record, but it captures them at a pivotal moment. They were living in a place that was still provisional in nearly every sense. Violence had only recently subsided. Streets wandered more than they ran. Merchants opened shops quickly and then disappeared just as fast. Saloons dotted Kansas Avenue. Topeka existed, but only just.

Jacob would argue a case in the morning, help raise a frame building in the afternoon, and spend the evening discussing whether the town would flourish or fail. Determination was everywhere.

Then came the force that changed everything: the Atchison, Topeka, and Santa Fe Railroad. Within two decades, the population of the wider region surged past 140,000. Ground once considered remote was suddenly tied to national markets, migration, freight, and the creation of new cities. What had been a hard frontier settlement was now embedded in a continental system, as steel rails opened Kansas to growth on a scale earlier generations could scarcely have imagined. And Jacob Safford was among the driving forces of that change.

Part 3 — A Nation Divided (1860 – 1880)

9

Billy Stealy

BY THE AUTUMN OF 1861, the rhythms of the Mackey farm had begun to feel fixed and inescapable. Billy had learned the habits of work, the language of seasons, and the acceptance of a household that had taken him in but never fully claimed him. Everywhere throughout the country, news was arriving in pieces: papers passed hand to hand, letters read aloud in general stores, and rumors traveling faster than fact. Men spoke of honor, of Union, of duty. Boys listened. Some listened more closely than others. There was talk of adventure, wages, and purpose.

The Mackeys had given him structure — chores before dawn, meals taken quickly, and sleep claimed when exhaustion allowed it. He grew stronger there. Leaner and useful. But usefulness came with its own expectations. He was never entirely a son, never fully a hired hand. Somewhere between belonging and obligation lay the narrow space he occupied.

War widened that space. Soldiers marched through nearby towns in uneven columns, boots kicking dust. Drums echoed across open fields, their steady rhythm carrying both promise and threat. Neighbors gathered in courtyards and churchyards to discuss enlistment. Some went for patriotism, some for wages. Others enlisted because the war offered escape from debts, grief, or futures that felt too small.

Billy watched. He listened. He understood that joining meant risk — injury, disease, the possibility of never returning. But he also understood that remaining meant continuing an existence shaped entirely by other people's decisions. He had been sent west. Assigned work. Given a room to sleep. War, for all its terror, offered him something the farm could not: a choice of his own.

On the morning he chose to leave, the farm looked much as it always had. September light lay thin over the fields, the first hint of autumn sharpening the air. Corn stood high and yellowing at the edges. Somewhere beyond the barn, a team stamped impatiently, iron shoes ringing against packed earth. It was the season of gathering and preparation, when labor intensified rather than eased. Leaving then meant abandoning not only labor but expectation.

Billy had risen early. Habit required no thought. He walked through familiar spaces — the rough boards of the loft floor beneath his feet, the smell of hay and leather, the low shifting sounds of animals waking to another day. For years, his days had been measured in such moments: harness buckles drawn tight, fence rails lifted into position, the steady pulse of a plow cutting forward under his hands.

When he walked down the lane that morning, he brought a change of clothes, perhaps his Bible or a schoolbook, and whatever coins he had managed to save. Behind him, the day continued its routines without pause. Smoke rose from the kitchen chimney. Livestock needed feeding, and the harvest would not wait. Whether anyone stood in the doorway to watch him go is impossible to know. What can be said is that when he finally reached town, he had crossed a boundary more significant than miles.

He was 14, although he wrote down 17, when he enlisted in the Union Army at Monmouth on the 16th of September, 1861. He entered not as a seasoned laborer or a trained soldier, but as a musician, one of the youngest roles recognized in Civil War regiments. Drummers and fifers served as the army's living signals. Their cadences governed the day: reveille at dawn, assembly calls, the cadence of marching columns, the advance or withdrawal on chaotic battlefields. He joined Company I of the 50th Illinois Infantry. For a boy accustomed to farm routine, the military's structure may have felt strangely familiar — another system of work and obedience.

Physically, he was still slight. At just over five feet tall, with dark hair and blue eyes noted in the descriptive muster roll, he would have stood smaller among men older and harder than himself. Yet youth itself was not unusual in the ranks. Many regiments contained boys who had stepped prematurely into adult roles, their presence tolerated because the war demanded numbers and because communities took pride in the eagerness of their young. The uniform he received did not quite fit. The drum straps cut into his shoulders. Some joked about his youth.

"Who enlisted the fifer's little brother?" one man called out.

"He's so small we'll lose him in the knapsack pile," another joked.

Illustration of Billy Stealy based on muster roll descriptions c 1864

A third grinned and tapped the drum. "No matter. We can hear him even if we can't see him."

Even the kinder remarks carried the same truth. "Keep close, Billy," an older soldier told him. "War's no place for boys."

Training blurred. The regiment formed around him like a moving village — farmers, clerks, laborers. Together, they stepped into a conflict larger than any single man could comprehend. Regimental musicians were not sheltered. Drummers marched prolonged distances, endured the same weather and shortages as the infantry, and often found themselves near the front lines.

In camp, they delivered messages, helped with the wounded, or performed routine duties assigned to any soldier. The drum was both instrument and burden — a symbol of purpose that marked them as essential participants in the army's daily survival. When Billy first marched, the drumbeat steady beneath his hands, he felt an unfamiliar emotion settle inside him. Purpose. He was not simply being moved forward by history. He was playing his own part.

In the initial months after enlistment, Billy's service bore little resemblance to the dramatic visions of battle that had drawn so many young men into uniform. The battalion proceeded through the disputed borderlands of Missouri and Kentucky, the terrain marked by dense hardwood forests, tangled underbrush, and rolling hills broken by steep ravines and muddy creek beds. Narrow dirt roads twisted through oak and sycamore groves, turning to deep mire after rain. Rivers and tributaries cut across the countryside in unpredictable passages, while patches of limestone outcrop and rocky bluffs slowed movement. It was terrain that favored ambush, where every wooded rise or bend in the road could conceal scouts, guerrillas, or enemy patrols.

Camps shifted frequently as commanders guarded rail lines, supply depots, and bridges essential to the Union war effort. Illness spread more efficiently than rumor. Dysentery, fever, and exposure thinned the ranks before musket fire ever did. Soldiers learned that endurance — not courage alone — would determine survival.

For Billy, these early campaigns were an education in discipline. He spent his days mastering the signals: the roll that summoned men from sleep, the sharp cadence that set marching columns in motion, the calls that marked drills repeated until movement became instinct.

He stayed near officers, watching how decisions were made under strain, how confidence could falter when reports from the front were unclear or when supply wagons failed to arrive. In these months, he also witnessed fear in its more subdued forms — men writing letters home by firelight, veterans of earlier skirmishes speaking in low voices about what real fighting would mean. Before he ever stood on a battlefield, he had begun to understand that war was not a single moment of glory but a slow process of hardening. This slow apprenticeship in discomfort transformed boys into soldiers, preparing them for the violence that would erupt at Shiloh.

Shiloh, April 1862

THE SOUND CAME FIRST. Distant thunder, irregular and unsettling, as if a storm were breaking somewhere beyond the tree line. Billy's hands rested on the familiar rim of his drum. He had practiced the rhythms until they felt like second nature. Forward. Halt. Advance. Order in the midst of chaos.

But nothing had prepared him for this. The officers' voices sharpened. Columns tightened. Somewhere ahead, smoke began to rise — not the clean gray of hearth fires but a thicker, dirtier cloud that clung to the ground. Men stopped joking. Conversations fell away. Even the wind seemed to hold its breath.

Illustration, Shiloh

Then came the crack of rifle fire. Instinctively, he flinched. The drumbeat started. His hands responded before his thoughts could catch up — muscle memory taking command where courage faltered. The rhythm provided the sense of order that would hold the regiment together as they advanced toward what none of them could fully see. Through breaks in the smoke, he glimpsed flashes of movement: blue coats, gray coats, men running, men falling.

The world narrowed. Sound became everything. Gunfire. Shouted commands and the dull thud of boots. The metallic scream of artillery somewhere beyond the trees. Billy felt the ground tremble beneath him as a cannon discharged, the concussion striking his chest like a physical blow.

He kept playing. That was his duty. That was the bargain he had made when he chose this path — to help guide soldiers forward even when forward meant stepping into madness. With each passing moment, the distance between boyhood and whatever came next grew thinner. A soldier stumbled past him, clutching his arm, blood darkening the sleeve. Another lay face down in the tall grass, unmoving, as though he had simply decided to rest. Billy forced his eyes ahead, focusing on the next beat, the next step. Survival depended on movement. A shell burst nearby, and dirt rained down. The battle surged around him, indifferent to fear and youth. The rhythm resumed — uneven now, but still recognizable — and the regiment pressed forward into smoke that swallowed them whole.

AFTER THE GREAT SHOCK of that April day, Billy's service gave way to two more grinding years of marches, sieges, and sudden combat as Company I of the 50th Illinois went deeper into the western theater of the war.

In the weeks after Shiloh, the regiment advanced with Union forces toward Corinth, Mississippi, where Confederate rail lines made it a strategic prize. There, Billy experienced the exhausting monotony of siege warfare—

digging entrenchments in oppressive heat, standing picket in swampy ground, and living amid sickness that killed almost as surely as bullets.

That fall, war returned in force at the Battle of Corinth in October 1862, when Confederate troops attempted to retake the town. Billy and his regiment were again under fire and joined the pursuit south toward the Hatchie River. These were brutal, disjointed engagements fought in powder smoke and confusion, where they marched hard one day and fought the next with little warning. When Corinth fell, the 50th Illinois remained there for extended stretches, guarding railroads and supply lines that were constantly threatened by Confederate raids.

Civil War Drummer Boys, Public Domain.

The winter of 1862–63 brought little relief. The regiment supported Grant's Central Mississippi operations and expeditions against Confederate cavalry under Nathan Bedford Forrest in West Tennessee. These campaigns meant grueling marches over ruined roads, scarce rations, freezing rain, and constant dread. Much of Billy's soldiering in this period consisted of breaking camp before dawn, crossing creeks in icy water, sleeping on wet ground, and guarding supply trains vulnerable to ambush. Men who had once struggled to shoulder their packs now marched with a grim efficiency born of habit.

In spring 1863, the 50th Illinois joined Dodge's expedition into northern Alabama, pushing through rough country around Tuscumbia, Town Creek, and Cherokee Station. These movements were meant to disrupt Confederate railroads and communications, exposing soldiers to a different kind of warfare: skirmishes in wooded ravines, sudden sniper fire from hidden ridges, and bridges burned behind retreating forces. By now, Billy was a veteran in the truest sense.

Later in 1863, the regiment shifted through LaGrange, Tennessee, then into northern Alabama again, moving through Eastport, Pulaski, and Lynnville. There, in November, the 50th Illinois was mounted, giving them faster movement through disputed territory. The change meant harsher weather conditions and extensive reconnaissance missions, with guerrillas and cavalry patrols posing constant threats.

In January 1864, after nearly three years in service, Billy mustered out. He left service, not as the boy who had first marched away in uniform, but as a seasoned soldier who had survived Shiloh, Corinth, months of occupation duty, repeated campaigns through Mississippi, Tennessee, and Alabama, and the slow attrition that wore down armies between famous battles. He had endured thousands of miles marched, seen comrades buried, and endured punishing cold.

He belonged to a regiment that had suffered heavy casualties. Official records show that the 50th Illinois had entered the war with roughly 1,000 men, including original enlistees and later replacements. It lost roughly 240 soldiers during its service.[1] Of those, only a portion were killed outright in combat or died of wounds; the larger share, as in many units, died from disease. Camp fevers, dysentery, pneumonia, typhoid, and other illnesses took men far more regularly than the Confederates did. One in four men who served with the 50th Illinois never came home alive.

Men were discharged for disability or deserted under strain. Some were captured and never fully recovered. Companies that had once marched out full of hometown faces were repeatedly thinned and refilled. Billy had changed from a young, frightened recruit into one of the war's weathered, but lucky survivors. The boy who had learned drum calls in muddy military camps was gone, and in his place was a seasoned war veteran.

His departure was not marked by ceremony. Equipment was turned in. Final pay accounts were settled, and the routine structures of the last three years loosened their hold.

The world he reentered, however, was at once familiar and irrevocably altered. The war was not quite over, but its effects were visible. Across much of the South, towns lay in ruins, farms were exhausted, rail lines were torn up, and the cotton economy that had once enriched planters was in collapse. Fields went untilled, labor systems had been shattered, and families on both sides were trying to rebuild from loss. The war had ended on paper more quickly than it ended in the lives of those who returned.

Cities in the north and west, meanwhile, had expanded, and railroads now extended further west. Labor was in demand, but not evenly. But the rhythms of civilian life felt smaller to Billy after years measured in marches, alarms, and the constant proximity of death.

Billy also took something from those years that could not be seen. He had watched friends fall beside him, heard the cries of men waiting for surgeons, and seen fields littered with the dead and dying. They knew the smell of blood, gun smoke, and sickness. Billy may not have borne obvious physical scars, but like many who survived, he held the war inwardly—its memories surfacing in silence, in temper, in restless nights, and in the private weight of things no one around him could fully understand. Though just in his late teens, his experiences during the war would set him apart from those who had stayed at home.

Billy did not go back to the Mackey farm. The war had given him wages and confidence. Now he would find work where it could be taken: in fields needing hands, along expanding rail lines, in river towns rebuilding after conflict.

By the late 1860s, he had drifted into northern Missouri, a region still recovering from the violence that had fractured it during the war years. Communities now sought stability, and families wanted husbands for daughters whose prospects had been narrowed by years of loss.

These Missouri communities were tightly woven. Church socials, parish gatherings, dances, and personal introductions formed the center of social activity. In an Irish Catholic immigrant circle—perhaps at Mass, a harvest gathering, or a neighbor's supper—Billy crossed paths with a young Irish woman, Kate Quinn. How they met is unrecorded; it may have been through kinship networks, which often brought newcomers and established residents together, or it may have been a chance encounter. Kate had recently arrived from Canada, her parents having fled Ireland during the famine of the 1840s. Their courtship progressed, and on November 2, 1869, Billy married Kate D. Quinn in Livingston County.

The union marked more than a personal milestone. Marriage finally offered Billy what the institutions of his youth — foster households and military service — had not fully provided: a future of his own making. He had a partner to share life's burdens and the hope that the instability of his early years might finally give way to permanence.

In 1870, Billy and his wife, Kate, were living in Trenton, Missouri, and he was no longer passing through. He was twenty-eight years old, and he had a trade: he was a barber.

In Trenton, that meant more than just cutting hair. The barbershop was one of the few regular gathering spots available to men across class lines. Farmers coming in from the surrounding countryside, laborers, merchants, local officials—they all passed through the chair. News moved there. Politics was argued there. Business was discussed during breaks, between customers, over the steady rhythm of his scissors.

"Take it shorter this time, Billy. My wife says I look like I wintered with the wolves," said one man.

"You did winter with the hogs, Sam," another man answered from the bench, drawing laughter.

A farmer shaking rain from his hat asked, "Corn's soft in the north fields. You hear if prices are holding in St. Joseph?"

"Prices hold for the banker," someone muttered. "For the rest of us, they slip."

Near the sink, politics began as it often did.

"Grant will do," said one customer. "Better than handing the country back to the men who broke it."

"And yet taxes keep rising," someone else replied. "Patriotism costs dear when the bill comes due."

Billy stropped a razor in long-practiced strokes and said little. Then the door opened, and a traveler stepped in with fresh reports.

"Railroad men are surveying west again."

"Surveying is free," came the answer from the bench. "Let me know when they lay iron."

The room laughed, argued, and went on. Hair fell to the floor in soft drifts while the town told itself what it believed.

For Billy, this occupation gave him a particular position: he was visible, known, and woven into its routines. The job required skill, but more importantly, consistency. Men returned to the same chair. Trust built slowly, then held. It was not a trade that would make a man wealthy. But it was one that could support a household.

And the household grew quickly. Daughter Margaret, whom they called Maggie, was born in 1870, followed by Maude, Agnes, and Harvey in rapid succession.

On June 12, 1873, Billy placed his name on an application for a Civil War pension as an invalid of the 50th Illinois Infantry. The war had ended eight years earlier, but for numerous veterans it persisted in their bodies as weaker lungs, aching joints, damaged hearing, nervous strain, what we would today call Post Traumatic Stress Disorder (PTSD), and pains that flared without warning.

Billy had been young when he entered the war, but youth was no guarantee against lasting harm. He had marched in rain and heat, slept on hard ground, lived amid disease, and witnessed violence at close range. He had seen soldiers broken open by shell and shot, and watched surgeons work with saw and knife. While some men came home visibly altered, there were those who carried their injuries where no census taker or neighbor could record them.

Billy's application suggests that the mechanics of ordinary life had become harder than pride alone could manage. Perhaps his hands stiffened at the barber's chair, or weakness came in spells. Perhaps nights brought little sleep, or the memories themselves wore on him in ways the government had no category to measure.

Whether the claim was approved is unknown. Many veterans were denied, delayed, or forced to prove again what war had already taken. What is certain is that he kept working.

By 1880, the young family had moved to Moberly, Missouri, a railroad community, more connected and more active. Growth came faster there, and opportunity with it. He was thirty-eight now, still working as a barber, still anchored to a trade that depended on the steady flow of people through town. The children, Magie, ten, and Maude, seven, were present and attending school. Education required stability—time away from labor and some level of predictability in income. In earlier years, especially in more unsettled eras, children's labor often came before schooling. Here, that balance had tipped. The family could afford, in time and structure if not in wealth, to invest in gains beyond the immediate needs of the household.

The address—Fifth Street—suggests an integration into its local fabric. Not on the margins or temporary, but inside the grid of a community organizing itself around Main Street, commerce, and routine. This was not prosperity in any expansive sense, but it was stability.

While the archive of his life offers only a glimpse—a fixed address, a defined occupation, and a young family—it tells us more. He was not drifting. Not laboring day to day, lacking an anchor. He had entered the middle of the nineteenth century, and after years shaped by movement— New York, Monmouth, the war, and the transitions that followed—this was different. A chair. A shop. And a town that knew his name. Billy had finally arrived at steadiness: a profession, a secure home, and children who were ready to move into the next generation.

---

[1] History - Illinois Infantry (Part - 4) www.civilwararchive.com

10

Jennie Safford

Topeka: 1861

Life in a Borderland

BY THE TIME WORD reached them—riders seen to the east, a farm taken, another burned—it was too late to decide whether it was rumor or truth. In Kansas, the difference did not matter. You prepared the same way either way. The ground behind the house was still soft enough to turn.

They worked quickly, digging just deep enough to bury only what could not be replaced. A small chest of the family silver and a stash of coins. Papers folded and tied. The things that proved ownership, held value, and that could not be brought if they had to run. There was no plan beyond that.

Inside, the house had gone quiet. Not frantic—just a tightening. Drawers opened, then closed. A few things gathered, most left behind. You did not pack for a raid. You chose what you needed to save.

The road was the only warning they had. Anyone could appear on it. Travelers. Neighbors. Or men armed and moving with purpose, progressing unannounced from Missouri into Kansas as they had before. Some came for horses. Some for food. Some for reasons no one could predict until they were in your yard. Stories arrived faster than riders. Each account slightly different, each one certain enough to be believed. As reports reached Topeka, the stories had done their work.

Jennie helped her mother cover the ground, pressing it flat with the back of the shovel, then scattering loose dirt and grass over it. There would be no marker. If they returned, they would have to remember where they had stood. If they returned.

"More to the left," her mother whispered. "There. Make it look as though nothing was touched."

Jennie kneeled and pulled at the grass with trembling fingers. "Will they come here?"

"I don't know."

"Then why bury it?"

"Because if they do come, we will have less to lose."

Jennie looked toward the house. "Couldn't we take it with us?"

Her mother gave a short, tired breath. "We can carry children or silver, not both."

The words settled harder than the shovel had.

Jennie pressed the earth again, trying to smooth away every sign. "How will we find it?"

"We remember that cottonwood, and that break in the fence line," she paused. "You must remember too."

Jennie nodded, though fear was making everything blur.

When the patch looked undisturbed, her mother straightened and brushed dirt from her skirt. "Say nothing of this to anyone."

"I won't."

Her mother touched her shoulder. "Good girl. Now go inside and help with the little ones."

From the yard, the vista stretched outward—open, exposed, lacking boundaries or protection. Somewhere beyond sight, riders were moving. Only the waiting remained.

From the yard, the vista stretched outward—open, exposed, lacking boundaries or protection. Somewhere beyond sight, men were coming. Only the waiting remained.

❖

A LETTER WRITTEN DECADES later recalled the fear of Quantrill's Raiders—irregular Confederate guerrillas whose movements through Kansas and Missouri left a trail of fear and reprisal. They buried the silver in a hurry. That single line in a letter written by Jennie's son, Ernest, reminded me that these were not distant events reported in newspapers. They were part of the everyday fears people lived with.

When the Civil War erupted, the violence intensified and spread across state lines. In Kansas, allegiances blurred, the law was unevenly enforced, and violence could arrive without warning. Looting parties terrorized the region. Farms were targeted, and towns were vulnerable. The distinction between civilian and combatant was not always clear.

Missouri also had fractured. Though it officially stayed in the Union, loyalties were divided, and by the summer of 1861, open warfare had begun. After early engagements, organized armies continued on, but the fighting did not end.

It changed form. Guerrilla bands operated independently, moving through rural areas and communities. They struck quickly and disappeared just as fast. There were no fixed fronts, no reliable protections, and little distinction between friend or foe. Neighbors could become enemies.

Out of this turmoil came William Quantrill, whose raiders were the most feared of these irregular forces. They roamed between Missouri and Kansas, targeting anyone and anyplace associated—rightly or wrongly—with the opposing side. The border war was shaped by a continuous exchange of retaliatory and counter-retaliatory strikes. People learned to watch roads, to measure distance, and to act on rumor because waiting for certainty could mean waiting too long.

This was the world in which Jennie Safford came of age. She was eleven when the Civil War broke out, and fourteen when it ended. There was little permanent infrastructure, and droughts could undo years of effort, reminding her that stability remained an aspiration. Wealth and influence did not insulate them from the region's volatility.

In 1863, Jacob Safford was 33 years old, and like many men of his age, he appears in Civil War draft rolls but did not serve. While soldiers marched east and south, he stayed in Kansas—where the war took a different form. Here, the question was not only who would win the war, but what kind of society would exist when it ended. However, the war did not leave the family untouched.

❖

SHE WAS BORN IN May 1862, at the edge of a country coming apart.

There had been hope in her arrival. In a time marked by enlistments and departures, a the birth of a child still carried the hope of continuity. Life insisting on itself. For a brief season, the war remained outside the walls of the home—spoken of, worried over, but held at a distance by the ordinary rhythms of feeding, sleeping, and watching a new life begin.

But the world she entered was not a gentle one. When Katie Safford, the third daughter born to Jacob and Esther Safford, arrived, Topeka was straining under pressures it had not been built to bear. By 1863, the war had drawn soldiers and supplies through its streets along with something less visible: disease. Typhoid, dysentery, and smallpox were not extraordinary episodes but constant threats that devastated households and encampments alike. There was no single moment when an epidemic declared itself. One day, it was simply there—first as a fever, then harder to deny. Sickness was embedded in the rhythm of a place living too close to war.

Infant lives, always fragile, were the first to give way. Sometime in July, just over a year after her birth, Katie fell ill. The symptoms would have been familiar: a temperature that spiked and then lingered, weakness that deepened, and a child who didn't respond as she had just days before. There were no effective treatments to turn to. Care meant presence—cool cloths, watchful nights, and the desperate prayer that strength might return. Sometimes it did. Often, it did not.

No record survives to name the infection. In truth, the distinction doesn't matter. The outcome was the same. Katie died in July 1863. She was 13 months old.

The record of her existence is brief, as so many were. A birth. A year. An ending marked more clearly in family memory than in official accounts. But her absence would have been anything but brief. Loss settled into the home, reshaping it in ways both visible and unseen. But losses would continue, and the fear was different the second time.

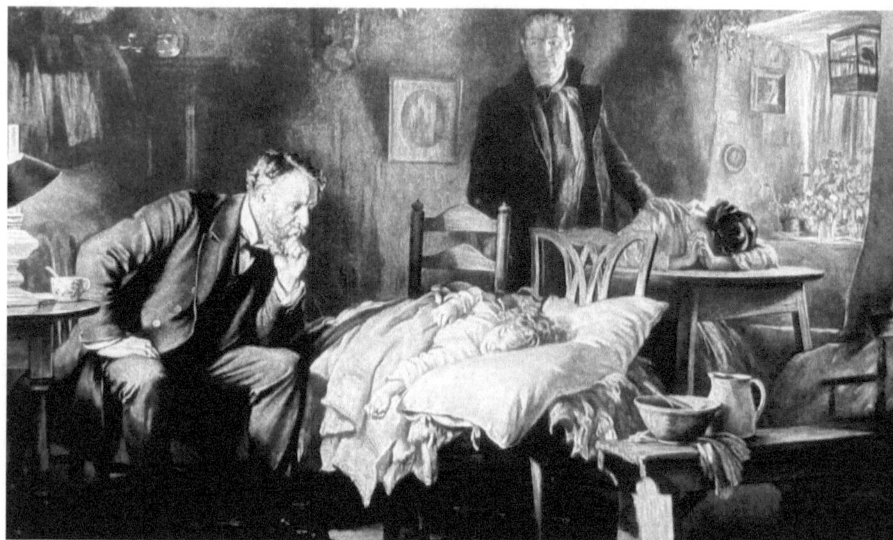

Illustration, Mary Safford

In September 1864, they faced it again when seven-year-old Mary fell ill. Her sickness shattered any remaining hope that the earlier death had been an isolated tragedy. Disease was now inherent to the world they were living in. That fall Mary died, one more nameless cause. And it would not be the last.

JENNIE STOOD JUST OUTSIDE the doorway. At almost 13, she understood more than anyone what was not being said aloud. She had learned to read the signs over the past two years—how voices lowered, doors shut, and the way adults behaved when things could not be fixed.

She had seen it before.

Her little sister's illness had appeared silently, then stayed. The memory arrived as a feeling—the waiting, watching, and how hope had narrowed day by day until there was nothing left. That had been only months ago. Before that, another loss. Each time, the house had shifted, but it had found its balance again.

This time, it did not.

Her mother had never fully recovered after the last baby came. Jennie could see it, even when no one said it plainly. There was a tiredness that did not lift, a stillness that seemed to settle deeper with each passing week. Some said it was weakness from giving birth or maybe a lingering illness that had taken hold many years ago and would not release its grip. Beyond the house, there were rumors of smallpox in nearby towns, of disease moving with soldiers and wagons. But inside, the cause mattered less than the awareness of what was happening.

Jennie stepped into the room.

The light was thin, pulled through the window and resting across the bed where her mother lay. Everything had been arranged carefully, as if order might keep her there. A basin. Cloths folded and refolded. A chair drawn close and then pushed back again.

Her mother did not move.

Jennie waited, expecting—out of habit more than belief—that there might be some slight sign, some recognition, some return. But there was none. The stillness was complete now.

Behind her, she could hear the baby, Charlie, stirring. Her little brother, only a year old, would not remember this day. That thought came to her suddenly, sharply. He would grow up without the memory of their mother's voice, her presence, or how she moved through the house, holding everyone and everything together.

Jennie would remember for both of them.

She did not cry right away. The emotion came differently this time: sadness settling into place, heavy and permanent. She knew that the house would go on. Meals would be prepared, and the baby would need tending. Her younger sisters could help, but as the oldest, her father would turn to her for help. They would keep on, but it would do so with something missing that could not be restored.

She stepped closer, just enough to see her mother's face clearly, committing it to memory as it was now—still, composed, beyond the reach of the illness that had taken her.

Outside, life went on as it always did. Wagons delivered goods. Voices carried. Somewhere, the war continued to grind forward. But inside the Safford house, time had narrowed.

❖

JACOB TOO WOULD HAVE to go on. And he did. Within a year, he remarried, and three more children were added to the Safford family: Henry and Dell, and later, Ernest.

Shortly after Esther's death, he joined the Kansas Supreme Court as its first justice, serving from 1865 to 1871. His portrait hung in the courthouse for many years after. On paper, this was the arc of a successful jurist. In practice, it was only part of the story. Jacob was drawn into the endeavors that were reshaping the state more visibly and more rapidly than the courts could: railroads, bridges, and regional development.

By 1868, he was serving as counsel to the Atchison, Topeka, and Santa Fe Railroad, which would become the main line linking Topeka to Kansas City. It was an undertaking full of risk.

❖

IN 1868, THE TREK east no longer required the same improvisation it once had. Rail lines now pushed steadily through the country, binding regions that had only recently felt distant. Jacob Safford was traveling with Cyrus Holliday, the founder of Topeka and eventually its Mayor. The two men were headed to New York, where their project's survival would be decided. It was their job to secure the funding that the Railroad needed. The visit was not ceremonial; it was necessary. The railroad in the years after the war was unstable, underfunded, and at risk of collapsing before it ever truly began. If capital wasn't secured, the line would fail.

Jacob Safford, c 1865

Jacob was well-suited for the mission. He was the kind of
man people trusted almost instinctively. Direct without
being harsh, approachable without sacrificing authority, he

carried himself with an easy steadiness that put others at ease. There was nothing theatrical about him; his strength lay in a calm, conciliatory manner that made him a natural mediator in rooms where stronger tempers often prevailed.

He had the gifts of a politician—good judgment, patience, and the ability to win confidence—but lacked the hunger for office that drives ambitious men. What distinguished him most was a quiet fairness: a habit of weighing matters carefully, listening before deciding, and approaching disputes with an honesty that made even opponents feel they had been heard.

The early miles of their journey were familiar: uneven roads, earth rising in dry stretches, and carriage wheels striking hard ground. But within a day or two, they reached the rail. And from there, the motion changed.

The train lurched, groaned, and pushed forward with steady mechanical insistence. Smoke poured back through the cars, settling into their clothes and hair. Windows were left open despite it. The seats were hard, and sleep crept in for stolen minutes, not hours. Conversation drifted in and out, alongside the constant metallic clatter of wheels over jointed track.

Missouri was followed by Illinois. Then, the line pushed east through Indiana, Ohio, and into Pennsylvania, with each connection intensifying the feeling of having entered a fully formed, rapidly progressing country. What had previously required weeks of rough prairie paths and deadly river crossings now took just days.

When they reached Manhattan, they had crossed from rural invention into something else entirely. New York in

1868 was noise, stone, and sheer velocity. Buildings rose five and six stories high, pressing inward. Faces of brick and granite crowded close along narrow streets, and horse-drawn omnibuses rattled past in constant movement. Drays hauled goods from the docks where laborers walked quickly, purposefully, with the rhythm of a place that measured time in money, not in seasons. The air held the layered smells of the harbor, animals, and industry.

Nothing paused. Commerce and movement had taken hold.

They dressed carefully. Not extravagantly, but with care. Dark wool coats, brushed and set as well as travel allowed. Waistcoats buttoned high and white shirts with stiff collars. Boots polished the night before, dust worked out of seams and creases. A cravat tied with attention. Hair trimmed. They understood the terms. They would be measured by every detail.

They made their way toward the financial district—Wall Street and its surrounding corridors, where money concentrated in counting houses and bank offices. Buildings were solid, permanent, and close-set, with narrow entrances leading into rooms lined with desks, ledgers, and men who dealt in numbers large enough to shape entire regions. There was the quiet scratch of pens, tall windows, and inside, a cool dimness compared to the street.

They paused at the threshold—feeling out of place for a moment. Evaluating themselves against the room. Their anxiety came from what they were here to ask for. Eastern financiers would need to put their faith in an idea not yet built: a railroad stretching through Kansas. This was not an established line with proven profits or a finished route linking mature markets. It was just an idea resting on belief: that people would continue pushing westward, that steel rails would lead and follow that movement, and that unsettled terrain would soon become essential to the nation's future.

Illustration, New York c 1868

They would have known how this sounded: speculative, distant, and risk-laden. The bankers in New York had heard frequent proposals just like this one. Railroads weren't curiosities anymore. They were instruments of expansion, and with that had come a flood of investment—and just as much failure. Lines had been overbuilt, claims exaggerated, and fortunes made and lost in rapid succession. Western routes weren't judged on vision alone, but on probability.

Kansas was not the only claim being proposed. It was one among many. Everything they had—political standing, personal reputation, the credibility of their town—was tied up in whether men in these rooms would agree.

It was not simply about financing a railroad: it was about securing Kansas into the national system of progress and expansion, or whether it would be left behind. Everything depended on the answer.

❖

THE 1868 VISIT TO New York marked a turning point for the Kansas railroad. Jacob Safford and the committee secured the investment, and what had been a struggling, tentative venture took shape. From that point forward, the project advanced with a momentum that surprised even its supporters.

Construction pushed outward from Topeka in measured, relentless increments. Mile by mile, town by town—until the line stretched hundreds of miles across Kansas and beyond. What had been empty terrain was connected space in a matter of years. Each mile completed altered the value of the surrounding ground.

The line began at Topeka in October 1868. From there, it pushed southwest in stages, each extension marking both distance covered and a claim laid on the future. The first towns connected were Burlingame, Carbondale, and Osage City, which were reached in 1869. Emporia and Cottonwood Falls the following year, and by 1872, the line reached Wichita. From there, the line extended further west through Kansas, all the way to Dodge City – a distance of 351 miles. By December 1872, the line had reached the western edge of Kansas—approximately 470 miles of track laid in just over four years.

More communities materialized, trade followed track, and distance shrank. The broader region took shape. And it was Jacob Safford who designed the legal and financial tools that made that construction possible—drafting legislation and securing county bonds. These were not small points. Without them, there would have been no railroad to build.

Then the Panic of 1873 sent the national economy to a halt, spreading financial ruin from coast to coast. Credit tightened again, and projects like theirs stalled or were abandoned entirely. The Kansas railroad was not insulated from this. Even though they were not operating from a position of strength, they carried on, aware that completion was improbable. But the work continued.

The railroad in Kansas today exists because they refused to let it fail. By 1880, the line reached Santa Fe and extended toward Albuquerque, eventually connecting with the Southern Pacific. What began as a regional effort was a continental network: one continuous network moving goods, people, and information over vast distances.

By the end of his career, Jacob Safford was remembered not only for his contributions as a judge but also as an "enterprising and public-spirited citizen" of Topeka. Even the landscape carries an echo of that influence. A Kansas community, Saffordville, bears their name — a reminder of how thoroughly some lives become embedded in the places they helped shape.

Judge Jacob Safford

On the third of July, 1885, at the age of 58, Jacob Safford died after a year-long battle with stomach cancer. He had held the inheritance of mobility, land, and belief—but had translated it into something new. Where earlier generations cleared fields, he helped establish courts. Where they marked boundaries with rivers and roads, he had helped define them in law. And where they went in search of opportunity, he chose to build a life in the center of one of the country's defining conflicts. He was, in that sense, exactly what the previous generations had been building toward.

✦

Jennie Marie Safford

Jennie's youth, her eldest son would later recall, was one of two vastly different worlds. During her childhood in the 1860s, the ground around her was still open and full of motion. There were seasons when the horizon seemed empty, stretched wide and quiet under a hard sky. And then there were days when it was alive. Herds passing in the distance—dark, shifting lines against the grass—so large they seemed to carry the earth with them. Years later, her son would remember her saying she had "ridden with the buffalo as a girl," a phrase that lingered somewhere between memory and myth. Whether she rode alongside them or simply rode near so that she could feel their presence hardly mattered.

Illustration, Girl and Buffalo

What she meant was clear: she had grown up when the world was still wild, still in motion, still incomplete. But the Saffords believed in refinement too, and a proper education, even for their daughters. Jennie became the second generation of Safford women to attend college, continuing a trend begun when her mother, Esther, attended

Oberlin. When she left for Bethany College in 1870, it was not an escape from the prairie so much as a refinement of it.

Safford Home, Topeka, Kansas

Bethany College offered structure, polish, and the sense of entering a broader world. It was, as she would later describe it, where she went "to get finished." Not finished in the sense of ending, but of shaping—learning how to move through rooms, through conversation, through a society that was itself becoming more defined. Music, language, deportment, and study. The rough edges of a pioneer upbringing were not erased, but they were softened. She held the memory of buffalo herds, the freedom of movement, and of a childhood spent where the future had not yet settled into form. That combination—frontier and finishing—gave her an understanding of both worlds.

When Jennie returned from college, Topeka had changed, and so had she. It was less raw, more structured, its future

189

beginning to take shape in rail lines and permanent buildings. She carried herself differently now, with the confidence of someone who had been prepared for the world beyond it. And she was about to step into her next role.

Jennie Marie Safford, c 1870

11

Ben McMeekin

Topeka, 1868

THE HOTEL WAS NEVER quiet. Doors opened and closed at all hours. Conversations echoed from the dining room into the hall. Even when he was sent upstairs, the sounds followed through the floorboards, through the walls, through the thin spaces where silence should have been.

His father owned the hotel. Standing at the center of it all, moving between rooms, speaking with those who treated him as an equal, H.D. was someone who belonged in that world of transactions and decisions. There were moments when Ben could see it clearly: the authority, the confidence, and how men deferred slightly when his father spoke.

The newspapers spoke of him as an old pioneer, a man whose past stretched back into the unsettled years of the early territory. Some accounts leaned into exaggeration—legendary river fights, improbable encounters with Natives, the kind of stories that grew in the retelling—but even stripped of embellishment, the outline was clear. His father had been present early, and he had stayed. Through the years, his reputation was not only that of a successful businessman, but also as what one account described as "the prince of landlords." He was even nominated for lieutenant governor. It was a long shadow to stand in.

Illustration, Topeka c. 1870

Ben was seventeen, and while he tried on the rhythms of his father's world, he never fully adopted them as his own. For awhile he worked beside H.D., learning the practical demands of the hotel trade: receiving travelers at all hours, overseeing supplies, tending to accounts, and making certain that the endless mundane crises of a public house did not become larger ones. But where his father took on these responsibilities with restless purpose—always building, negotiating, and looking toward the next civic opportunity—Ben stayed at the edges of the action. He was present, dependable, and known, but never the driving force. Where H.D. saw the hotel as a platform from which to shape a town, Ben drifted within it; a man formed in the shadow of louder personalities, participating in their world but not eager to command it himself.

The political conversations that animated his father and so many of Topeka's prominent players continued to swirl constantly around him in the hotel parlors, but to Ben, they were background noise rather than a personal calling.

That difference may have been owed to temperament and also to the environment in which he was raised. The hotel was a predominantly male arena where business, politics, and alcohol flowed together almost inseparably. In the public rooms of the lodge, whiskey and brandy were part of the daily fabric of conversation. Alliances were reinforced by rounds poured freely, and it was commonplace for respectable men to drink heavily in ordinary society.

My great-grandmother Mabel recalled that "to be known as a 'two-bottle man'" was quite common in that era and did not necessarily mark someone as what we would now call an alcoholic. It could even carry a certain admiration: a man who could hold his drink in a culture where evenings of liquor, cards, and masculine endurance were ordinary social currency.

Ben had grown up in that atmosphere from boyhood, surrounded by the clink of bottles on polished wood, cigar smoke hanging low beneath gaslight. Everything was discussed over whiskey, grievances aired over beer, gossip shared round by round. To keep pace at the table was, for many, a measurement of being counted among men.

Topeka, too, was growing up. After decades of turbulence, the town was settling into its next phase of prosperity. In 1870, it was the state capital and held 5,800 people. The streets were alive with the steady movement of wagons, horses, and pedestrians from dawn until well after dusk. The city spread outward from Kansas Avenue, its main commercial artery, where merchants' signs swung above board sidewalks and storefront windows displayed bolts of cloth, farm tools, imported china, and dry goods brought in by rail.

The arrival of the expanding railroad lines had changed the pace entirely. Freight cars now delivered lumber, machinery, and eastern-manufactured goods in quantities once unimaginable, while rail connections linked Topeka to Kansas City, where travelers and goods were transferred onward to St. Louis, Chicago, and the larger eastern network. Residents still relied on horse-drawn buggies, carriages, and omnibuses for daily transport, but more people now walked the streets graded for heavier traffic, where the noise of iron-rimmed wheels and hoofbeats echoed off rows of newly built brick buildings.

Most of the earlier frame structures had given way to substantial brick business blocks, inns, warehouses, churches, and government buildings, their facades rising two and three stories above the muddy streets. The Kansas Statehouse, still under construction, stood as a visible declaration of purpose, its unfinished grandeur signaling Topeka's intention to become more than a regional outpost.

Residential neighborhoods stretched beyond the commercial center into streets lined with modest clapboard cottages, boarding houses, fenced gardens, and larger homes belonging to merchants, lawyers, and railroad officials. Cottonwoods and young elms had begun to shade the avenues, softening what only a decade earlier had been raw prairie ground.

Topeka now reflected both industry and sociability. Women shopped in millinery stores and attended church socials; men gathered in public house parlors, saloons, and lodge halls to gather news and share reports from other towns. Blacksmith shops rang with hammer blows, printing presses ran steadily, and schoolchildren filled newly established classrooms as families put down roots. On market days, farmers from the surrounding countryside arrived with produce, eggs, butter, and livestock, filling the city with country wagons and trade. Evenings brought lectures, musical performances, debating societies, and public meetings, evidence of a place increasingly concerned not merely with survival but with culture, reputation, and civic identity.

Ideology, too, was always present. While Ben had been raised in a household where slavery politics had once been argued as fiercely as land claims or elections, he came of age in a different Kansas—one less consumed by the political clash and more concerned with rebuilding, trade, and stability. If H.D. represented the era when men fought to determine what Kansas would become, Ben belonged to the generation that accepted the outcome and turned toward making a living inside it. His joining the openly Free-State Saffords may also suggest that whatever partisan loyalties shaped his childhood had either softened, evolved, or ceased to define him.

It was against this background that Ben met Jennie Marie Safford, and the course of two histories began to converge. Until 1871, the McMeekins and Saffords had progressed along separate tracks: the McMeekins had built their position in Kansas through enterprise tied to the raw society of a growing territory: roadhouses that served as centers of lodging, drink, political bargaining, and commerce. The Saffords, by contrast, had established themselves through law, finance, and public leadership, their influence felt in courtrooms, railroad promotion, and the deliberate civic planning.

Perhaps they met in the hotel lobby, where the transient and the established crossed paths—local families passing through on errands or social calls. Or perhaps it was through simpler channels: an introduction, a gathering, a connection through the fledgling but growing networks of a town becoming a city. What the record preserves is that Ben McMeekin and Jennie Marie Safford were married in Topeka on a spring day in 1872. He was 21 and she, 19. And from that union a new family emerges, and the story continues—west again.

Recreation of Kansas Avenue north of 6th Street, Topeka, 1870

12

Ben and Jennie

LAWRENCE REMEMBERED THE HEAD. Mounted high on the wall of the hotel lobby, it seemed enormous—dark glass eyes fixed in a permanent stare, the heavy curve of the horns casting far shadows depending on the hour of the day. Adults passed beneath it without looking. To them, it was a decoration or a trophy that belonged in a room where men came and went carrying money, news, and dreams.

But to a child, it was alive.

Lawrence stood beneath it, small enough that the polished wood of the lobby counter rose above his line of sight. He had learned where to stand to avoid being noticed. From there, he could watch the room but not be pulled into it—the visitors arriving dusty from the road, voices loud and confident.

Once, lifted up as a kind of joke, he had been placed on Ben's shoulders beneath it. He could feel his father's hands holding his legs, steady but not entirely still.

"Go on," someone had said. "Let him try."

He reached forward, hesitant at first, and touched the coarse hair on the animal's neck. The room responded with approval—laughter, encouragement, the easy noise of men who found nothing unusual in the moment.

Lawrence would never forget its cold, black eyes.

IN 1872, THE MCMEEKIN and Safford families were joined when Jennie Safford married Benjamin McMeekin. The match linked two trajectories: one rooted in organized power, the other in the earlier, more volatile phase of settlement. The couple settled in Topeka, where Ben took a role at the McMeekin Hotel. Together, they had two children: Lawrence, who was born in 1873, and his sister Esther, whom they called Essie, born in 1876. Outwardly, it was the continuation of a stable, upward-moving family. But the reality was more complicated.

Letters and recollections describe a household marked by volatility. Benjamin struggled with alcohol, common for his day. Tensions were not hidden so much as endured—a typical response in a period when divorce held a biting social stigma and silence was often the chosen response.

"Ben was a hard drinker. In those days all men were though. If you weren't a two bottle man, you weren't a man at all, you know. He owned a hotel... [Lawrence Safford] said his earliest memory, in fact his only memory of his father at all was that there was this great mounted buffalo head in the lobby of his hotel, and that his father used to delight in putting Lawrence up on this head which would send him into hysterics, as he was terrified of the beast."

– Mabel Power Chamberlain, 1970

One day, Jennie made her decision. She shifted from room to room decisively. Drawers opened and shut. A valise lay open on the bed. Folding children's clothes first, then stockings, shirts, a comb, important papers, and a few photographs. Not everything—only what mattered. The rest would remain where it was.

"Lawrence," she called from the bedroom. "Come here a moment."

He appeared in the doorway, still small enough still to look upward at every adult question.

"Yes, Mama?"

She knelt beside the case and brushed a strand of hair from his forehead. "Go to your room and bring me two or three things that you love."

He frowned. "Why?"

"Because we are going away."

"For how long?"

She paused only a second. "Long enough that you must choose carefully."

His face displayed confusion. "Is Father coming?"

"No."

"Is Essie coming?"

"Yes."

"Is Rufus coming?"

Jennie paused. She hadn't considered bringing the dog. After a moment, she responded. "Of course, Rufus will come too."

That seemed to brighten Lawrence's eyes for a moment.

He looked past her at the half-packed room, trying hard to understand what children are asked to understand too early.

"But why are we going?"

Jennie drew a breath. "Because sometimes a house stops being a place where children should stay. And when that happens, you must know when to leave."

He stood silent, absorbing words too large for him.

"Now go on," she said more softly. "Bring what you love. We cannot take what is heavy, only what is dear."

He returned with a toy, his favorite book worn at the corners, and some personal treasure that no adult would have chosen. She carefully made room for it all.

Jennie Safford with son Lawrence Safford (McMeekin) Chamberlain

When it was time, she took his hand and lifted the case. Lawrence watched the rooms as they passed through them, sensing that something larger than furniture was being left behind. There were no words that could have made sense of it. No attempt to soften what could not be softened. She simply gathered him as she gathered everything else—with intention and finality.

It was 1877. They left the building the same way others did every day. Through the front, into the light, past the same door where guests came and went. There was nothing outward to mark the difference between departure and routine. But for Lawrence, the world had shifted. He would not return to that life. The hotel and his father remained. The mounted Buffalo head still watched over the lobby, unchanged. But he was no longer part of it.

He did not know what would replace it, only that it was gone. The separation of his parents did not just alter a household. It redirected his life.

In 1884, Jennie remarried to Philander Chase Chamberlain. With that decision, the family's identity changed again. In that era, children were absorbed into new identities. Surnames—especially when associated with divorce— were simply erased. What had been the McMeekin name was never spoken of again. It occurred in how they were introduced, listed, and presented in the community. The earlier name fell into disuse. The past was erased. No one ever spoke of Ben: his name did not appear in memory, in story, or in the casual recounting of family history. In fact, the McMeekin name faded so completely from memory that in later years even Mabel could not recall her husband's biological father's name; only a fragment of identity, maybe that he had been an Irishman from Kentucky.

Lawrence Safford (McMeekin) Chamberlain, age 9

The McMeekin children, Lawrence and Essie, grew into adulthood under the surname Chamberlain, and with that came a different alignment—socially, legally, and generationally.

Lawrence's life was steadier than the one his parents had fought to secure. The raw hardships of the frontier had receded from daily experience and become family lore— stories told at tables and on porches about hunger, danger, wagers taken, and fortunes nearly lost. He was born into the aftermath of struggle rather than the struggle itself.

He never knew Kansas as a violent borderland or an uncertain rumor on a map. By the time he came of age, it was a place of schools, offices, churches, and civic ambition. Education could confer standing. A profession could shape identity. Advancement didn't depend on holding a rifle or staking a claim, but on learning how to navigate the foundations of a maturing town.

But families knew that economic success could still vanish with changes in railroad traffic or agricultural markets. Political alliances required maintenance. Reputation mattered. Parents who had witnessed settlements rise and fall in a single decade taught their children to value both progress and caution, to pursue advancement while preparing for unexpected reversal.

From this layered legacy—of prominence, instability, and reinvention—emerged Lawrence Safford Chamberlain. With his younger sister and two new siblings, he remained at 317 Clay Street, the two-story brick house in Topeka where their blended lives continued under one roof. Jennie, whose hair had turned white as snow while still in her twenties, brought a gentler influence to the household and encouraged in him a love of art and literature.

Lawrence carried more than one legacy. From the Saffords came standing, discipline, and public expectation. From the McMeekins came restlessness, intensity, and the unresolved fractures of an earlier household. Neither line was simple, and neither disappeared. They met in him, as histories often do—as temperament, instinct, and unspoken habit. This is how patterns endure: not only in stories told, but in what descendants inherit without being asked.

Part 4 — An Age of Arrival (1880-1900)

13

Maggie Stealy

❖

Moberly, Missouri —1885

THE GROUND WAS HARDER than expected.

They had begun digging before sunrise, their breath visible in the cold air as shovels struck frozen soil with dull, repetitive force. Missouri winters did not arrive gently.

Kate Stealy stood apart from the gathering, her gloved hands folded tightly at her waist. She had been a wife for fifteen years. Long enough to have settled into the rhythms of their household together: the steady routines of the barber's trade and the optimism that hardship, once endured, might give way to something more assured.

The coffin was plain.

There had been no money for ornament. Friends and neighbors had done what they could, contributing labor, food, and small gestures of solidarity that marked both compassion and the practical limits of their community. Death was familiar here. It came through illness, accident, or exhaustion. People mourned and went on.

Kate had been born far from Missouri, in the northern communities of Perth, Ontario, where Irish emigrants had attempted to rebuild lives disrupted by famine and economic forces. Her parents, Patrick Quinn and Isabella McGee, had left County Cork, Ireland, in search of a permanent home in British North America. When she married Billy in 1869, she had internalized the frontier lesson that days were never guaranteed.

The children shifted uneasily beside her. Maggie, at fourteen, was old enough to understand there was a finality to what was happening, but too young to grasp what it would really mean in the years ahead. They both stared fixedly at the box being lowered into the narrow space cut from frozen earth.

Somewhere in the distance, a train whistle sounded. Kate watched until the first shovelful of dirt struck the lid. The sound was heavier than she expected. Billy Stealy's life, marked by famine, orphan trains, and war, was drawing to a close not amid a dramatic battle but through the simple labor of men who would go back to their farms before midday.

She thought of the stories he rarely told. Of New York streets crowded beyond imagination, an island where children learned to wait for decisions made by others, and the trek west that ultimately had driven him to what they had tried to build together. The memories were now a shared inheritance, a blend of his past and the stories she would need to tell.

Snow began to fall.

It settled on the turned soil, then on shoulders, hats, eyelashes. Kate knew that survival would once again depend on adaptation — on finding work, relying on kin and neighbors, and making choices that balanced necessity against expectations. Within a few years, she would marry again. Not because grief had diminished, but because her daily reality left little room for solitary survival. The decision reflected neither weakness nor betrayal. It reflected the determination to ensure that the family Billy helped create would not dissolve into the same institutional instability that had marked his own childhood.

She took a breath, turned from the grave, and walked toward what still demanded her attention.

The past had carried her husband west. Now it would carry his children forward.

❖

Margaret "Maggie" Stealy, 1888

MAGGIE DID NOT REMEMBER the day her father was buried, only remnants that remained with her in the years after—images without sequence, perceptions that settled into memory more as feeling than fact. Her mother kept certain objects with deliberate care; items that seemed to carry more significance than they should. But her days demanded attention elsewhere.

Morning light meant chores. It was Maggie's job to fetch the water. And it was daily physical labor. Every household needed a fresh supply for drinking, cooking, washing, and bathing—and someone had to haul it. Families usually relied on private or shared wells, cisterns, hand pumps, or nearby streams. A bucket lowered by rope into a well was common, and later, iron hand pumps made lifting water easier. Rainwater was often collected from roofs into cisterns and used for washing or laundry.

Inside the home, water was carried in by hand and stored in pitchers, crocks, barrels, wash basins, and kitchen reservoirs. Morning chores required several heavy buckets.

Baths were heated on a stove and poured into a tub. On laundry day, significant quantities of water, both hauled and heated, were needed, making it grueling labor for women and children as the men worked.

Waste disposal was equally primitive. Outhouses, privies, chamber pots, or cesspits created constant sanitation problems. Wells could be contaminated if set too close to waste pits, a common cause for the spread of diseases like dysentery.

Maggie was also responsible for her younger siblings, and school was not to be missed. But the house itself was changing, too. Her mother did what she had to do. Lots had been sold, rooms were rented, and strangers moved through the house: men with trunks, with jobs that sent them in and out of Kansas City, and voices that did not lower at night. The home that had once been theirs was now given to others: a boarding house, a business, a space shared and negotiated. Meals were no longer just family. Privacy narrowed. Routine shifted to accommodate people who were passing through.

Maggie was seventeen now and aware that stability could be lost without warning. What she didn't anticipate was her mother's remarriage.

A new man in the house, but not in the same way. Authority returned, but it did not restore what had been lost. It rearranged things. Her mother's bedroom door was now closed and off-limits. New rules imposed. A new center of gravity was forming, and everyone was expected to orbit it.

For Maggie, it carried a particular sting. Teenage feelings have little standing in times of crisis. Her grief, jealousy, and confusion were secondary to rent, reputation, and practical needs. She was not yet free to choose her own life, only old enough to be keenly aware of the choices being made for her.

Leaving home began as a calculation—private and internal. Weighing what options existed and where she could go. Imagining what it would mean to stay, and what it might mean to step outside the life that didn't feel like hers anymore. Marriage, at that age, was not just about attachment: it was a way out. A chance to move from one household into another where her position might be more secure, more hers. Not necessarily easier—but chosen, at least in part, rather than imposed.

When she left, it didn't feel sudden to her. It felt like the only direction that remained.

14

Mabel Power

Moberly, Missouri—1889

MAGGIE STEALY WAS 18 and did not arrive that night expecting to meet her future husband.

Community dances served multiple purposes in those days. They marked seasonal transitions, celebrated modest successes, and offered young people a rare opportunity to imagine lives beyond the routines that governed their days. That evening, benches were cleared, the hall was cleaned, and lantern light softened the rough edges of the unfinished walls.

In the corner was a piano. Its varnish bore the scars of travel, its keys uneven in tone. But when Maggie sat down to play, the instrument became a bridge between worlds. Music allowed her to move beyond the regular daily demands.

James Michael Power noticed her before he knew her name. He had grown up in England in a household where music, education, and refinement mattered. Even as he navigated the uncertainties of building a future in America, traces of his upbringing remained in his posture and how he evaluated his surroundings.

Seeing Maggie at the piano disrupted whatever expectations he had formed about the night ahead. Music shaped the moment. Both were pianists, and both had connections to a conservatory, reflecting a shared cultural ambition. In an era when technical skill and artistic refinement were often intertwined, the piano could signal education, aspiration, and emotional sensitivity all at once.

When he joined her later in the evening, the conversation started cautiously. Shared skills provided an opening. They spoke of composers, teachers remembered, and of the Irish and Welsh ballads that had survived migration. Each recognized the other's history, shaped by movement.

When they parted that night, each carried away the private excitement of a relationship just beginning to stir—the flutter of wondering when they might meet again, and whether the spark they had felt was shared. There was in it the sweetness of new hope, that tender, unsure exhilaration that comes when one life suddenly seems poised to open into another. The evening felt as if some unseen door had quietly swung open, and both had stepped toward a future neither yet dared to name.

Later, Maggie received a note. Written on a scrap of paper, bordered with a spray of violets, the kind of inexpensive but sentimental stationery popular then. The letter was brief—an apology and a brief mention about a returned item. Maggie kept it. The image is telling. A young man holding onto a small, intimate token of an evening's companionship.

Years later, her daughter Mabel asked what it was he had been so reluctant to give back. Maggie answered simply: her dancing shoes. They had been left behind in the excitement of that night—forgotten, or perhaps not entirely by accident. He had held onto them longer than necessary, as if they carried her with them. Returning them required more than the errand itself.

And then, shortly afterwards, he came back again—this time with no pretense of borrowed things, and no intention of leaving empty-handed. The decision to marry followed quickly by the standards of their day. Youthful resolve often took precedence over extended courtship, particularly when economic opportunity and social expectations intersected. Stories would later circulate that they had run away together, choosing faith in each other over the careful approval of relatives who worried about class, stability, or reputation. If such tensions existed, they were not unusual. Maggie knew that love alone could not secure a household, but she also recognized in James a partner capable of navigating the forces that were reshaping the nation.

What is certain is that on a summer day in July 1889 in Jackson County, Missouri, James Power and Maggie Stealy were married by a Justice of the Peace, and together they stepped into a future neither could fully predict. She was 18, and he, 24. Maggie had graduated from high school only weeks before.

He had left England when he was 18, in dramatic fashion as a stowaway on a Banana Boat. The story Mabel told my father—that he ate so many bananas he could not bear the sight of one for the rest of his life—turns out to be true. He arrived in Iberia, Louisiana — a Gulf Coast community where immigrants and itinerant workers frequently began again with little more than their skills.

Misfortune seemed to follow him. A fire destroyed his personal papers, erasing much of the documentary trace of his early adulthood. Like many of his generation, he rebuilt through work, reputation, and sheer persistence, crafting an identity not from preserved records but from the industries he helped bring into being and the family he ultimately led.

Illustration, Missouri c 1880

By the late 1880s, he had wandered to Missouri, where his future started to take shape, including the life he would build with Maggie. For their generation, the sound that defined America wasn't the crack of musket fire or the creak of wagon wheels. It was industry. Farms were being replaced by factories, and rural living was increasingly being traded for bedroom communities.

Their household would stand at the intersection of multiple relocations — Irish famine survivors, orphan-train children, industrial English workers — each story

216

contributing to a broader narrative of how ordinary people navigated the transformations of the nineteenth century.

Sometime between their June marriage and the following spring, the couple transitioned to Kansas City, Kansas. It may have been opportunity, it may have offered a larger and more reliable industrial base—steady pay in the shops and yards that smaller towns could not sustain—or simply the pull of a place already thick with people like them, building lives out of the same tenuous beginnings. Their first child, a daughter whom they named Mabel Lucile, was born on a spring day in April, 1890, in Kansas City. Siblings Olive and Walter followed in quick succession.

By 1900, the Powers had reached a point of measurable security—modest, but hard-earned. James was a machinist — a skilled industrial trade that placed him in the emerging middle class of American labor. These were men who did not own factories but understood how to build, install, and maintain the gears that powered them. Refrigeration was still a developing technology, its possibilities not yet fully embraced.

Businesses that depended on reliable storage—meatpackers, grocers, dairies, and transport companies—were beginning to invest in innovative systems that could stretch both time and distance. Before refrigeration, families and shopkeepers relied on cellars, springhouses, salting, smoking, pickling, and blocks of winter-cut ice packed in sawdust to slow spoilage. These methods, however, offered only brief protection and limited success. The arrival of icehouses on a larger commercial scale, followed by primitive mechanical refrigeration units, transformed that equation.

Meat could be shipped farther without spoiling, milk lasted longer in city markets, and produce no longer had to be consumed almost as soon as it was harvested. What had once been governed by season and immediacy was now subject to human control. The ability to preserve perishables was one of the silent marvels of the industrial age.

For a man willing to travel, install equipment, and solve problems wherever he was needed, the field offered both employment and professional identity for James. He went where contracts demanded, sometimes for weeks at a time, to cities and industrial centers where refrigeration systems were reshaping commerce.

Letters were traded for conversations. Travel became routine. Their household balanced domestic continuity against the demands of professional determination.

A decade later, they were living in Ward 6 on Miami Avenue, a rented house in a growing working-class district shaped by rail lines, stockyards, and industry. James was listed as head of household, naturalized, and steadily employed as a machinist. There were signs of strain: he reported two months of unemployment within the year—a reminder that even skilled tradesmen were not immune to the fluctuations of industrial labor.

Mabel, now ten, and Olive, seven, were attending school. The presence of Maggie's brother, Harvy Stealy, who was nineteen, suggests that extended kin networks still mattered. His inclusion in their home reflects the common practice of shared households as both an economic fallback and a means of social connection.

They did not own their house, but rented. Yet everything else suggests forward motion: a skilled occupation, a stable marriage, surviving children, and literacy: this was not a family in crisis. They were in progress—rooted now, and building something that, while not wealthy, was secure.

Mabel recalls that he occupied the unquestioned, and typical for its era, role as head of the house. Authority rested with him; decisions passed through him, and the comfort of the women under his roof was part of a man's duty. James could be firm in manner, but he also believed women were to be indulged, protected from rough burdens when possible, and treated with a certain ceremonial regard; they were to be "spoiled."

"Maggie, you've set this out finer than any hotel in town," James remarked as he took his seat at the dinner table.

"Oh, Papa, it's only a roast and cobbler for dessert. Thanks to you, we have fruit!" Mabel said with a smile.

James waved the correction aside. "Nonsense. If my wife wants peaches in winter, she shall have peaches in winter."

He helped himself, then turned his attention toward his daughter. "My dear, will you be going to visit Cousin Harry on Saturday?"

"Yes, Papa."

"A young lady may certainly go," he said, pausing for effect, "provided she remembers she bears the Powers name—and keeps better company than her father ever did."

He mixed authority with affection and command with performance. If Maggie lifted something heavy, he would rise immediately: "Leave that. I've not kept a house so my women can do a laborer's work." Or if Mabel seemed cross, he might soften at once. "Now, who has displeased you? Point him out, and I'll have words."

It was paternalism, certainly, but of a common kind for the era: a man who believed women should defer to male authority while also being shielded, flattered, and fussed over. In his mind, rule and tenderness were not opposites. They were the same obligation.

Within a few years, the Powers had moved west to Coronado, California, a coastal community that was half resort and half speculative promise. It was a long move from Kansas City, and like many families at the turn of the century, they had followed the pull of the West, where climate, growth, and prospects drew people outward in steady numbers. By 1920, his lengthy involvement with refrigeration had resulted in a more established position. Listed as an erecting engineer for a refrigeration plant, he now owned a home at 761 "C" Avenue in Coronado, just down the block from his daughter Mabel and her growing family. Ownership marked a turning point.

For an immigrant who had once lost personal papers and all his possessions, holding property signified permanence. His career had shifted from itinerant installations toward technical supervision and responsibility.

The 1940 census lists him as a widowed father-in-law living with Lawrence and Mabel Chamberlain on the same Coronado avenue where he and Maggie had lived. He was seventy-seven, and the arc of his life — from stowaway youth and wandering mechanic to property owner and family elder — reflects both the volatility and the prospects of his era.

James Michael Power died in San Diego on July 2, 1943. His story, stitched together through census entries and scattered recollections, reveals a man shaped by movement, industry, and persistence — one of countless immigrants whose technical labor silently underwrote the modern American landscape.

❖

MABEL AND HER SIBLINGS grew up hearing bits of stories that stretched backward: England to America, Ireland to New York, from the city to the prairie. However, their daily experience was markedly different from that of their grandparents. Schooling was expected, and local infrastructure was reliable. Books were valued in the home, and education suggested possibility. Music — inherited from both Maggie and James — offered refinement as well as pleasure. While many children still grew up measuring success through land ownership or manual skill, Mabel's environment encouraged attention to culture, memory, and self-presentation.

The hardships that had shaped Mabel's grandfather, Billy, receded into anecdote, then into legend. Younger generations heard the lore and internalized the lessons: the readiness to move if opportunity demanded it and the belief that progress lay somewhere just ahead. In this way, the legacy of being carried west became the capacity to choose where to go next.

Part 5 —Dawn of Modern Days (1900s)

15

Lawrence Chamberlain

Topeka, 1900

LAWRENCE SAFFORD CHAMBERLAIN'S CHILDHOOD unfolded in a household where stability and expectation were present in equal measure. Lawrence's stepfather moved in two influential worlds: the law office and the newspaper room. One dealt in statutes, contracts, and public disputes; the other in opinion, politics, commerce, and the daily pulse of the city. For a teenage boy, it was an education far beyond the classroom.

A lawyer's household exposed him further to the language of civic organizations that his grandfather, Jacob, had occupied. Courts, property, civic order, and reputation were matters of importance. He knew that advancement depended not only on hard work but on understanding how systems functioned and how respectable citizens carried themselves within them. When his stepfather entered the newspaper trade, the lesson widened. Newspapers were engines of influence in the nineteenth century, shaping elections, promoting business interests, attacking rivals, and telling citizens what mattered. The Saffords engaged in lively conversations about public affairs, local personalities, and prospects.

This early education in civics helped create a man who was later comfortable in banking and local leadership and held a respected public standing.

His half-brothers, Phillip and Ernest, were born shortly after his mother's marriage to P.C. Chamberlain in 1885. As a teenager, he was energetic and athletic, a young man who loved baseball and played in a Topeka league. In the game, he found both camaraderie and escape, until the demands of adulthood gradually forced him to set aside bat and glove for good.

In academics, the sciences held particular appeal. Medicine, emerging as a profession defined by training and recognition, offered both financial security and social status, as well as the ability to contribute to community well-being. The era of self-made frontier generalists gave way to specialized expertise. America was professionalizing. Doctors, engineers, teachers, and lawyers formed networks that extended beyond individual towns.

Topeka was more modern now, too. Horse-drawn wagons still crowded the roads, but beside them were electric streetcars carrying clerks, shoppers, and office workers across town with speed and routine. Kerosene lamps and candles were converted to electric lighting, first seen in businesses and wealthier homes along the avenues. Evenings no longer ended abruptly at sundown. Stores could remain open later, offices functioned after dark, and parlors glowed with a steady light far cleaner than smoke-blackened lamps. The marvel of telephones, still a novelty at first, linked homes, banks, and businesses. Messages that once required a ride to the other side of town or a hand-delivered note could now be spoken in moments.

Domestic living was growing easier as well. Indoor plumbing, running water, furnaces, and improved stoves meant homes were warmer and life more efficient. Ice delivery and early refrigeration improved food storage. Ready-made clothing, mail-order catalogs, and department stores also offered conveniences that his mother, Jennie, could scarcely have imagined.

For Lawrence, the changes were astonishing. He had been born in a border settlement with a violent history. By middle age, he was living in a world connected by wires, rails, and electric light. The modern era had unmistakably arrived. His generation would determine whether that stability could be sustained — and how the restless movement that had shaped so many families might grow into a modern future.

His mother would often share recollections of river landings choked with mud, elections disrupted by gunfire, and the relentless winters of homesteaders. The stories were both warning and inspiration — reminders that the security they enjoyed had been built on risk and persistence.

Lawrence grew into adulthood balancing these legacies. He valued formal schooling, yet respected practical knowledge. He sought advancement but didn't abandon the pioneer ethic of adaptability. He chose the University of Kansas Medical School and graduated in 1898. His progress was swift.

He attended the Mayo Clinic for his postgraduate studies, and in 1906, he had risen to become Superintendent of

Christ Hospital in Topeka — an achievement that marked him as a young physician of unusual discipline and administrative promise. He had also married a fellow medical student, Olive Lewis, just three years earlier. But their intended life together would not unfold as they had hoped.

Lawrence Chamberlain, c 1893

❖

Topeka, 1906

LAWRENCE KNEW BEFORE ANYONE said the word.

Pregnancy was meant to be a hopeful condition, a forward-looking one. But the winter had not been kind to Olive. At first, the changes seemed ordinary: the way she gripped the chair arm and how the swelling in her hands had deepened—not dramatically, not yet, but enough to see that her rings didn't fit how they should. She had begun to take them off to relieve the discomfort. That was when he understood. And as the months passed, he noticed a heaviness that settled over her even on bright mornings.

Lawrence was 33 and had been a physician for the last eight years. He had spent years studying the subtle language of the body, the slight betrayals that signaled deeper disorder. Olive's brilliance had always been present in her quick decisions, gestures, and an alertness that filled whatever room she entered. Even as she tried to keep her routine, to receive visitors, and discuss cases with the cool authority that had distinguished her at medical college, she would have seen the signs too. She knew, beneath the surface, that a battle was underway — one neither of them could bring themselves to name.

Olive was not merely his wife. She was his equal. Educated, disciplined, and ambitious in ways still rare for women at the turn of the century, she had completed advanced medical training with confidence and was popular in Kansas's social and academic circles.

It had not been easy. While women in medicine in 1905 were not unheard of, they were still unwelcome. The lecture halls were filled almost entirely with men who had grown up believing that medicine was not simply a profession but a masculine calling. They spoke of endurance, authority, and scientific mastery, leaving little room for women except as patients or nurses. A woman who insisted on asking questions and mastering anatomy and surgical technique was seen not as a colleague but as an intrusion.

They called her a "hen medic." It was meant to be clever. Dismissive. A phrase tossed into corridors and dissection rooms with a half-smile, an insult meant to reduce her to something domestic and ridiculous. The implication was that women might imitate the motions of the profession but could never truly belong inside it. To them, she was performing medicine, not practicing it.

Every successful exam, sound clinical choice, and healed patient was an argument stronger than anything she could say. She put in more hours than most of her peers, aware that any errors she made would be seen not as personal shortcomings but as evidence of women's general unsuitability for the field. But she did not complain.

Her marriage to Dr. Lawrence Safford Chamberlain in September 1903 had seemed to provide a partnership defined as much by shared professional ideals as by affection. They were part of the modern world.

When labor began, it came too early. Olive had insisted on remaining at home. It was what women did. Hospitals were wards of infection and a last resort. At home, she could control the environment and remain in familiar rooms. The irony was not lost on anyone present: she was a doctor herself, trained, capable, accustomed to being at the bedside of others. Now she lay in the narrow space between professional ability and bodily peril.

The household was roused in the dark. Lamps were lit, and towels warmed. The familiar choreography of turn-of-the-century childbirth unfolded with practiced urgency. Lawrence shifted between roles, at once physician and husband; his training guiding his hands even as his heart rebelled against the necessity of clinical detachment. The house was full of medical attendants — a strained gathering who understood too well what might unfold behind the closed bedroom door. Childbirth was still a borderland between science and prayer. Even for physicians.

On the front steps, the waiting became unbearable. Her father was there. Her brother was there. Everyone sitting in uneasy silence, hats in their hands, words trailing off as broken thoughts. The night stretched. Inside, movement could be heard — hurried footsteps, low instructions, the creak of the bedframe, and the muted urgency of people confronting what they could not command.

Olive bore the pain with disciplined endurance. There were moments when her composure faltered — confusion, and waves of nausea that left her trembling. Her pulse ran irregular beneath his fingers. The swelling that had troubled him for weeks had worsened. He recognized the signs now with terrible clarity. Something was wrong far beyond the mechanics of birth.

The child arrived tiny and weak, its initial cries thin and tentative. They wrapped the baby carefully. They watched for breath, movement, and the assurances that physicians and parents alike sought in the first vulnerable minutes after delivery. But the newborn's struggle was evident.

Too early. Too frail. The rhythms of breathing never fully steadied. Lawrence did what he could, though he understood how little the medicine of his era could offer her. Premature life existed on a narrow margin that skill alone could not widen.

Meanwhile, Olive slipped further away. Her exhaustion deepened into a more ominous state. He monitored her as a physician would, aware that the body could become its own enemy when vital organs failed to perform their silent duties.

Uremia. The word contained an awful clarity. The body poisoning itself when the kidneys stopped performing their labor. He understood the likely progression and, in a distant professional sense, the limits of intervention. What he could not accept was its presence here, in his own home, beside the woman who shared both his vocation and his future.

He had read the case studies and even debated such outcomes in lecture halls where tragedy remained theoretical. Now he watched as his medical training offered knowledge but not the remedy. The toxic accumulation progressed. The tools they required — dialysis and a kidney transplant —were decades from existence.

They tried what they could. When the door finally opened, no one needed the words.

She was gone. The baby had not survived.

For a long time, no one spoke. The assurance of medical training had collapsed in a single room. Olive, who had held patients' lives in her own hands, had been overtaken by the oldest risk of womanhood.

Later, Mabel would remember how Lawrence described the scene: the men all huddled together on the porch, stunned into stillness. She remembered, too, how Lawrence came to the bitter realization that even a house filled with doctors could not guarantee survival. He was a doctor. Her brother was a doctor. She was a doctor. And there was nothing any of them could do.

At that moment, he said he wanted nothing more to do with medicine. He had devoted himself to preserving life. For a physician, there is a particular kind of devastation in witnessing the limits of one's own profession. While he did return to his profession briefly, it was never his passion again.

In the days that followed, condolences filled the rooms. Friends spoke of a promise interrupted and a life barely begun. Lawrence, who had spent years training himself to act — to diagnose, decide, and intervene — found himself instead confined to the role of witness. He signed certificates instead of prescriptions and endured empty comforts. What unsettled him most was not only the loss but that he had understood the danger as it unfolded. He had recognized the signs, grasped the trajectory, and still been unable to alter the outcome.

In the years that followed, he would carry that sense of powerlessness. At first, he didn't want to go on. Eventually, he would find a way.

Mrs. Olive Lewis Chamberlain and infant daughter, Olive Lewis, died at the Chamberlain home, 414 Harrison street, Topeka, yesterday. Mrs. Chamberlain's death was caused by uremic poisoning. The funeral will be held on Saturday morning from the home in Topeka.

Mrs. Chamberlain was the second daughter of Dr. J. P. Lewis and wife. She was born on May 2, 1876, at Pleasanton, Ohio. She came to Topeka in 1882. Mrs. Chamberlain was highly educated. She graduated from the Topeka high school in 1897 and from the school of pharmacy of the State University in 1899. In February, 1902, she graduated with honors from the Kansas Medical College. She was married September 1, 1903, to Dr. Lawrence Safford Chamberlain.

Mrs. Chamberlain was well known here and was very popular among her student friends during her university career. She was an exceptionally good student in her college work.

She was a member of the Ladies' Shakespeare club, the Art club and the Kappa Kappa Gamma sorority. She was very prominent in the social life of Topeka, had a wide acquaintance and leaves a large number of friends.

Mr. Chamberlain is physician for the Esperando Mining company in Southern California. Mrs. Chamberlain has been in Topeka since last May.

Obituary for Olive Chamberlain, 1906

❖

AS A WIDOWER AT 33, restless, alone, and searching for direction, Lawrence looked toward the coast. Southern California, with its expanding cities and capacity for renewal, offered the possibility of a fresh start. The Pacific coast suggested both escape and possibility, a setting where personal loss might be softened by environment as much as by time. Lawrence would go west.

The Desert Appointment

The train did not go all the way to the mines. It left him instead at a sun-bleached siding where the wind blew freely over miles of pale sand and broken rock, carrying with it the metallic smell of blasted earth. Beyond the single platform stood a water tank, a freight shed, and a scattering of men whose clothes were the color of the country itself — dust-toned, stiff with salt, and worn at the seams.

Dr. Lawrence Safford Chamberlain stepped down from the coach, his physician's black case in hand, a new focus closing in around him.

He had come west not as a prospector or a gambler, or a man fleeing debt, but as a more modern man— an employee of a corporation whose aspirations were buried beneath the desert floor. The Esperanza Mining Company had retained him as its physician, a position that offered good wages, professional advancement, and the chance to grieve alone.

The mine promised riches that few would ever hold in their hands. Investors in distant cities read reports filled with tonnage estimates and projected yields. Lawrence would learn to read other signs — the tremor in a miner's hand before collapse, the gray pallor that preceded hemorrhage, and the quiet resignation of those who understood the desert might keep them.

Nothing in his years of study in Kansas had prepared him for the vastness of Southern California's mining districts.

Here, the distances were deceptive. A ridge that seemed an hour away might take half a day to reach. A camp marked on company maps was usually little more than canvas tents pinned to the ground by determination alone.

The wagon that met him was loaded with blasting powder and crates of tinned food. He climbed aboard beside the driver, who nodded once in greeting before urging the team forward. The road, if it could be called that, coiled through a landscape that appeared both ancient and freshly wounded — hills carved open by picks and dynamite, tailings piled like fresh graves, and skeletal stamp mills whose iron jaws groaned through the oppressive afternoons.

Men toiled everywhere. They swung sledgehammers against drill steel and shoveled ore into rattling carts moving in slow, deliberate rhythms beneath a sun that seemed intent on reducing flesh to residue. Accidents were inevitable. The company knew this. That was why it had hired him.

When they reached the camp, Lawrence understood his duties would extend far beyond the neat confines of a consulting room. He would treat crushed limbs and powder burns, and lance infections born of dust and poor water. He would fight fevers that ravaged bunkhouses crowded with transient laborers from half a dozen nations. He would certify deaths.

In the evenings, after the machines fell silent and the desert cooled with astonishing speed, he sometimes stood outside his quarters and looked east toward a horizon he could no longer see. Somewhere beyond it lay the ordered streets of Topeka, the lecture halls where he had mastered anatomy, and the social expectations of a profession that still imagined itself as a guardian of civility. Here, civility was negotiable.

It was in this harsh proving ground of speculation and endurance that his western experience began — and it would carry him from isolated camps of blasted slate to the polished civic rituals of coastal California, where initiative wore linen instead of cotton and fortunes were measured in influence instead of ore.

The desert, however, had marked him first.

———————————◆◆———————————

HE TOLD HIMSELF IT was exhaustion.

Mining camps did that to a man. The hard rides over broken ground, the nights spent bending over improvised operating tables, the constant smell of powder smoke and crushed rock — all of it accumulated in the body in ways that no medical text fully described. Lawrence had grown thinner in the desert, more deliberate in his movements, but he attributed the change to grief and overwork. There were always more patients than hours. Always another injury waiting beyond the next ridge.

Then the cough appeared.

He noticed it one evening while writing notes by lamplight in his quarters. A dry irritation at the back of his throat. He paused, cleared it, and continued. Outside, the mill pounded with mechanical persistence. Fine particles hung in the air even after dark, coating boots, bedding, and his medical instruments. It found its way into the lungs. Weeks passed.

The cough did not leave. It deepened. Sometimes it woke him before dawn, pulling him from uneasy sleep into fits that left his chest aching. He measured his own symptoms with the same detached precision he had once applied to his patients. Appetite diminished. Strength lagged. Fever came and went.

He knew its most likely cause. There were too many men in camp claimed by the disease, men he had treated. He had listened to their breathing grow shallow. Tuberculosis was an occupational reality — an invisible companion to blasting powder and falling stone. Physicians were not immune. Still, he believed himself strong enough to resist it. He had to believe that.

The confirmation came one morning. He rose early, the desert light lifting from shadow. As he dressed, the now-familiar tightening seized his chest. He leaned against the washstand, waiting for it to pass. It did not. The coughing came harder than before, each convulsion sharper, more insistent. When he finally straightened, there was blood on the handkerchief.

There was no panic. Only recognition. Years of training compressed into an instant of irreversible understanding. Hemoptysis — the clinical term surfaced automatically, absurd in its neatness. He had written it in charts for others. Now he was confronted with its reality.

He finished dressing. Doctors did not have the luxury of immediate collapse. He rode out that day, treated an injured foreman, and returned to his quarters with the same measured composure he had always shown. But the private calculus had begun. He couldn't pretend this was fatigue alone. The desert days, the sand-filled wards, and the close contact with miners who had the same illness — all of it had exacted its price.

By the time he sought formal consultation, the verdict only confirmed what he already knew. It was called 'consumption' for what it did to the body. The recommendation was predictable: rest, dry climate, and distance from strain.

For many Americans, and like his grandfather before him, the prescription was sunlight and clean air. The Southern California coast had become full of boarding houses with consumptives who spent their days reclining on verandas and measuring progress in ounces gained or lost.

He made arrangements.

To colleagues, he spoke of recovery. To himself, he admitted a harsher possibility. He had watched countless patients follow this path to imagine easy reprieve. Yet the decision to go to the coast held clarity. If he were to decline, he would do so under salt air rather than in the suffocating confines of camp.

The train left the mines at daybreak. Ahead lay San Diego — a locale spoken of in equal parts sanctuary and last resort. He did not know which it would prove to be. But he was certain of one thing: the future he had once planned had ended. Whatever remained would have to be built from what the illness might allow him to keep.

"He went out West to die."

Many years later, when asked why Lawrence came to California, Mabel spoke bluntly. "He came out here to die." The phrase held neither theatricality nor self-pity. It was simply the most honest explanation he could offer for abandoning a life that had seemed carefully constructed only months earlier.

Olive had died. His daughter had died. Tuberculosis was taking what was left. Whether he lacked the will or the physical strength, when he arrived in San Diego around 1908, he expected to be buried within the year.

But something else happened entirely: he lived.

❖

Consumptive Wards —Baja, California, 1908

THE HOUSES WERE BUILT for air. Wide porches wrapped around them, their railings lined with reclining chairs whose occupants spent extended afternoons facing the sea. There was a peculiar seriousness to the routines of the sick. Each morning, attendants brought the wicker chairs into the light. Patients were settled in rows, wrapped in shawls, even as the day warmed. Blankets were folded with care across thin legs. Conversations were polite and subdued, so as not to disturb the balance being negotiated inside their chests. They read papers weeks out of date and wrote letters that grew shorter as days passed. A few simply watched the sky with the intense concentration of people who had been given too much time to think. Thermometers were shaken and read. Milk was sipped slowly. Every small act was a quiet campaign against time. Lawrence took his place among them.

By the turn of the century, San Diego had begun to acquire a reputation — not merely as a resort, but as a refuge. The salt air drifting inland from the Pacific was said to strengthen the lungs. The mild winters offered reprieve from the damp chills that haunted eastern cities. Hotels reinvented themselves as sanatoria. Boarding houses advertised "sun parlors" and rooftop sleeping decks where the afflicted could lie beneath covered awnings and listen to the muted crash of waves.

Lawrence had once been the man who moved among bedsides with authority. Now he measured his own strength in increments — the distance he could walk without coughing, the appetite he could summon, or the steadiness of his hands when he opened a medical journal he no longer knew if he would practice from again.

At dusk, the verandas filled with a different kind of silence. The sea breeze cooled the day's warmth, and the air held the faint scent of kelp and tar from the harbor. Lamps were lit behind lace curtains. Somewhere, a piano might be heard playing a tune that felt both hopeful and unbearably nostalgic. On certain evenings, patients who felt strong gathered to discuss improvements that might or might not prove real. Weight gained. Fever reduced. A night slept through.

Here, recovery revealed itself slowly, almost shyly, in the return of color to a face or the decision to walk a little farther down the bluff road. Death, too, was announced without spectacle. A chair might remain empty one morning. The routine adjusted. But Lawrence remained.

Whether by resilience, chance, or by the same mysterious calculus that had already taken so much from him, he did not follow the path many had come west anticipating. The ocean air filled his lungs. Time — the one remedy no physician could dispense — started its silent work.

In this suspended world—balanced between ending and beginning—the future arrived without announcement. It was closer than he knew.

16

Lawrence and Mabel

—————————————————◀◆ ◆▶—————————————————

Coronado, California: 1913

BY 1913, LAWRENCE CHAMBERLAIN was no longer living in the shadow of loss.

He had survived tuberculosis and began to look for his next opportunity. He arrived in San Diego around 1912. From there he traveled across the bay to Coronado, where he encountered a different tempo — one shaped not by hospital corridors and professional disappointment, but by sunlight, ocean breezes, and the small but insistent demands of a growing coastal community. Meeting Mabel Power also altered his trajectory.

How that happened has been lost to time. Perhaps their paths crossed at the Hotel del Coronado, in its dining rooms or along the wide terraces where visitors and residents shifted easily between leisure and introduction. Or perhaps it was more ordinary—a chance encounter, or through the mundane and repeated intersections of daily living: across the counter at the general store or a merchant. Or simply walking on the street.

There's no record of how they felt about what they were embarking on. But on the 31st day of May, 1913, Mabel Power and Lawrence Safford Chamberlain were married in Coronado, California. She was 23, and he was 39.

Wedding Announcement for Mabel Power and Lawrence Chamberlain

Their union introduced possibility when Lawrence had expected a life alone. Marriage did not erase grief, but it redirected purpose and offered reentry into a future he had once struggled to imagine. The years that followed Olive's death and his recovery had been marked by an inward reckoning. But, now, purpose returned.

His work once again mattered in the community, and his name began to circulate in the same social networks that organized charitable efforts, public improvements, and respectable civic activities. They purchased a home on "C" Avenue, just a few doors down from Mabel's parents, situating themselves within one of its established residential corridors. The house was a center of activity: visits from colleagues, gatherings with local organizations, and the ordinary but meaningful rituals of domestic society.

In 1916, their only child, Jane, was born, an event that deepened Lawrence's sense that he had at last pushed beyond the doubts of earlier years. Parental responsibilities and community obligations soon filled their days. The rhythms of school terms, town meetings, and professional duties created a structure that gradually displaced the silence of past grief. In Coronado, Lawrence and Mabel were no longer defined by what had been lost. They were becoming part of what was being made.

Coronado, too, was just beginning its story. Founded in the 1880s as a resort community, the Hotel del Coronado was its focal point, drawing visitors and settlers from around the world. Getting there from San Diego, however, still required a commitment. There was no bridge yet, so from San Diego the trip meant a ferry ride over the gray-green harbor water, watching the low skyline of warehouses and masts fall behind as the wide, flat sand spit of Coronado grew larger. Wind pushed salt air and the metallic tang of shipyards. There was the sound of gulls wheeling overhead and the deep, booming calls of foghorns drifting in from Point Loma.

By the 1910s, the place was filling in with residential bungalows like theirs, adding to neat rows of orderly neighborhood streets. In 1913, the assembly line was introduced by Henry Ford, changing the course of transportation in America, and two years later, the first transcontinental telephone call linked New York and San Francisco. America was entering the modern age.

By 1916, the population of Coronado was 4,500 people. The Chamberlain home didn't represent luxury like the great estates being built along Ocean Boulevard, the grand hotel district, or the speculative beachfront tracts: theirs was a middle-to upper-class neighborhood where Coronado's permanent residents were beginning to anchor themselves.

The streets were not the tight, shaded corridors you see today. Pepper trees and young palms had been planted optimistically but had not yet grown into canopy. Between houses, you could see tight empty lots, scrub growth, wind-flattened weeds, sometimes laundry strung between posts. Much of central Coronado was just sand beneath thin wagon-furrowed roadbeds. Some sections featured early cobblestone paving or oiled surfaces. Boardwalk sidewalks ran in uneven lines.

Coronado Mailman, 1913. Public Domain.

On "C" Avenue, fresh Craftsman bungalows lined the street — modest, confident houses built by local contractors and small investors who believed Coronado's future was secure. They shared a common language of low-pitched gabled roofs, wide, sheltering porches supported by square

wooden posts, and shingles still sharp with the smell of
fresh paint. Rough plank borders edged the front yards.

They sat on narrow lots — twenty-five or fifty feet wide
— giving the block a rhythmic pattern of house-yard-house-
yard stretching toward the cross streets. Behind most of the
houses stood simple detached cottages or sheds —
washhouses, rented rooms, and future guest quarters. The
idea of a house as a compound was common. Families
expected growth, boarders, and change.

Some homes were softened by use, others were so new
that the surrounding soil was still raw from recent grading.
The street was not silent. A hammer echoed from a half-built
porch, accompanied by the distant sounds of children
yelling or a phonograph or a radio playing softly from an
open window.

There were even cows still being kept down the street at
360 "C" Avenue – to the displeasure of the neighbors and
Lawrence and Mabel. There were occasionally stray horses,
burros, and mules found wandering. The Polo Club found a
unique solution for trimming grass and weeds: 29 guinea
pigs were purchased and turned loose on the grounds,
which delighted residents and guests.

There were cars, too, but only a few. In 1913, the
automobile had arrived, but it had not conquered the street.
Most households did not own one. Delivery wagons from
San Diego merchants rattled up and down the streets, and
bicycles leaned against porch railings, while occasionally a
Model T was left parked at an angle near the curb. Lawrence
and Mabel watched this transformation closely — the slow

replacement of hooves and wheels by combustion and rubber.

Their home was modern. It had electric lighting, indoor plumbing, built-in cabinets, and a lustrous clawfoot bathtub with a deep enamel finish. Rooms were compact but intentional, with the parlor facing the street, dining room behind, and a narrow kitchen at the rear. There was a sleeping porch in the back for summer nights. This is where Lawrence would spend his last days, nearly fifty years later, smoking cigars and listening to the ballgame on the radio before he passed away at home in 1965.

❖

The War Years

IT STARTED WITH THE sound. Bugles in the mornings and engines. Not the sputtering noises of Model Ts, but the heavier, more industrial sounds from North Island.

Aircraft and training flights. The low thrum of motors testing themselves against marine wind. On certain days, the sky itself seemed to hum. Sailors in fresh uniforms moved constantly along the streets, walking in pairs and groups, laughing too loudly, carrying satchels, and writing letters on front steps while waiting for rides back to the ferry. Coronado wasn't simply a seaside town. It was a military village.

Throughout World War I, the detached cottage at the rear of Lawrence and Mabel's lot was rented out to sailors. Space was scarce, and the Navy presence was growing faster than housing could keep up. Men came and went — some staying weeks, some only days. They had the restless energy of people waiting to be sent somewhere else.

Lawrence was now active in local civics and political activities. When the dailies described him as a 'clubman,' the word had a meaning far deeper than simple social membership.

In the early twentieth century, a clubman was a man who had crossed an invisible threshold. More than just a resident or businessman, a clubman was someone integral to the inner social machinery — the network of relationships through which decisions were made, opportunities were introduced, and reputations confirmed.

The clubs themselves consisted of reading rooms and luncheon tables, shaded galleries and smoke-filled card rooms. Leather chairs worn smooth by years of conversation. Financial journals folded open to financial pages, the faint clink of glassware, and the steady murmur of men discussing land, shipping schedules, bond issues, or the future of the Navy's growing presence over the bay.

To be seen as a clubman suggested comfort in these settings. Lawrence was comfortable in both the modest residential streets of Coronado and the more polished spaces where influence gathered. He understood how transactions were made, trust was built, and how contracts began not with papers but with repeated encounters — a nod across a dining room, a handshake on the balcony of the Hotel del Coronado, or a quiet conversation after a Rotary luncheon.

His social status put him at the center of Coronado politics. In an era before formal political machines or

modern campaign strategies defined local leadership, clubs
functioned as informal clearinghouses of authority. Here,
merchants met bankers. Developers met naval officers and
civic boosters measured one another's reliability. A man's
presence alone signaled that he belonged to the class of
citizens expected to guide the town's future.

For Lawrence, this was the result of years invested in
establishing trust within a community that valued
reliability. A clubman was dependable, discreet, and
invested in the future prosperity of the place he called
home. In Coronado, this status mattered enormously. To be
a clubman was to be a man whose voice mattered when
questions of development, taxation, or civic direction arose.
It was an identity earned over time, through presence,
participation, and the belief that he would be there when the
town needed him.

That year, he was elected President of the recently
formalized City Council — still sometimes called the Board
of Trustees — a circle of practical businessmen tasked with
managing a town that was growing faster than its
infrastructure could keep pace. He would serve as President
from 1918 until 1924. Coronado did not formally use the title
of mayor, but the office Lawrence held was its equivalent.

Council meetings were not grand affairs. They were held
in modest rooms lit by electric bulbs that hummed faintly
overhead. Papers were spread over heavy wooden tables:
maps of future street improvements, tax assessments,
proposals for sewer extensions, and park maintenance.
Lawrence listened more than he spoke, his Kansas-born
steadiness making him a useful mediator between

competing visions for its future. The job was practical, immediate, and often thankless. Developers wanted expansion while residents wanted quiet. Merchants wanted better roads and worried that unregulated rentals or poorly maintained streets might discourage the well-heeled visitors whose winter stays sustained the local economy, while homeowners worried about taxes.

The men on the council knew each other well. They passed each other daily on Orange Avenue, in bank lobbies, at church socials, and in the hallways of the Hotel del Coronado. Governance here was less about ideology than about reputation. He might spend the morning negotiating ferry schedules or improvements, knowing that Coronado's connection to the mainland was both its lifeline and its vulnerability. Any disruption could ripple through shops, boarding houses, and bank ledgers alike. Its reputation as a refined seaside destination demanded careful protection.

Naval expansion brought its own contradictions. The presence of sailors meant business for property owners and shopkeepers, but also strained infrastructure and unsettled long-time residents who remembered Coronado as a more peaceful outpost. Zoning disputes were increasingly personal, argued not in distant offices but across fences and over supper tables. Guest cottages multiplied. Landowners saw opportunity. Neighbors saw disruption.

Simultaneously, great hotels and their investors expected cooperation, believing Coronado's future depended on preserving its image as a refined seaside escape. Beneath all of it ran the restless energy of speculation. Lawrence found himself mediating between optimism and caution, desire and stability.

Mabel's days, too, were intersecting with expanding roles for women, shifting class expectations, and her role as mother to a young daughter. Her hours were seldom idle. Coronado's social scene was built around calling cards, reputations, visits, and calendars. Mabel was central to that world. She knew who was related to whom, which family had standing, who had married well, who had slipped socially, and which names still carried weight. For Mabel, social knowledge was a form of currency, and she amassed it fluently.

With young Jane beside her, Mabel spent her afternoons with the rituals of society's expectations: lunches with other women at the Hotel del Coronado, charity teas, church functions, musicales, garden gatherings, and school entertainments where mothers watched children recite lines or perform simple plays. Jane accompanied her through neighbors' parlors, hotel courtyards, verandas, and shaded streets, learning early the rhythms of adult conversation and public manners.

The Great War also created a need for women to run patriotic drives, Red Cross work, and rationing appeals. Yet daily living continued. Dresses and hats were chosen with care, invitations answered, gossip exchanged, and luncheon tables set. If anything, such rituals often were more important in uncertain times, preserving a sense of order and continuity.

Mabel was thriving. She was not an idle or ornamental woman. In an age before social media or television, women like Mabel were what held communities together. Her active social life was not the only thing that set her apart. Household labor and the arts were not separate realms for her. While standing at the kitchen sink, hands submerged in suds, dialogue or scene might suddenly take shape. She would pause, shake the water from her fingers, reach for a pencil, and quickly jot down the thought before returning to the task. These notes — urgent, imperfect, but necessary — became the raw material of her creative expression.

In an era before sticky notes, scraps of paper accumulated wherever her day happened to unfold — pinned to curtains, tucked into table coverings, fastened to whatever piece of cloth or furniture was closest at hand. Inspiration was not scheduled; it was something she captured before it disappeared.

When the house finally quieted — when Jane was asleep, and Lawrence had gone out to a ball game or to play golf — Mabel turned those fragments into finished productions. In those narrow windows of solitude, she wrote one-act plays that cemented her own standing in the local arts community. Over the years, she wrote dozens of plays, several of them prize-winning works, and her comedies and one-act creations were staged repeatedly at local playhouses for more than a decade, acknowledging her talent as a playwright in her own right.

The creation of those theatrical productions seemed almost improbable given the conditions under which they were produced. It reflected her discipline as much as her skill: she did not wait for ideal circumstances, she made use of whatever time and space existed.

Those who observed her saw both the fortitude and the confidence it required. Around her, while conversations continued, Mabel kept working, building a creative world from notes pinned to curtains and ideas rescued from the rush of ordinary days.

She was proud of the resilience that her family had endured through decades of upheaval and determined to claim a place within a modern society that increasingly measured worth through cultural fluency and personal initiative. In this way, she was both product and architect of change. She carried her mother's love of music, artistic pursuits, and educational initiatives and occupied a world where identity could be curated rather than merely endured.

❖

1920s – 1930s

LAWRENCE STARTED HIS DAY as he always did, with a precision that was his public identity. He was a "top hat to - tails" man, never without a fine pocket watch or a walking cane. He had chocolate brown hair and piercing eyes so dark they appeared to be black.

Inside the Federal Savings and Loan, the air was cool and smelled of oiled wood. Depositors removed their hats when they saw him. Banking and governance blurred together in Coronado. Loans financed cottages, and those cottages became rentals. Rentals filled with newcomers to the coast. Growth was outpacing ordinances.

Evenings were spent sitting on the front porch with Mabel and Jane. As the fog crept inland, softening the edges of roofs and telephone wires, porch lights flickered on one by one. Radios, increasingly common, murmured through open windows. The porch witnessed the moments when he set aside civic responsibilities and simply watched dusk settle over a town he had helped shape. More than just somewhere to sit, it was an extension of society. A place to be seen and where neighbors stopped to talk.

Lawrence Safford Chamberlain, c 1910

By the 1920s and 30s, the rhythm of Lawrence Chamberlain's days had changed in ways that would have astonished the younger man who had once arrived without aim or hope in San Diego in 1908.

But the true center of Coronado — especially for a man in business and civic circles — was not on C Avenue.

It was at the Del.

The Del Coronado

On certain afternoons, Lawrence would make the short drive or even walk toward Orange Avenue, the great wooden mass of the Hotel del Coronado rising ahead of him, its red roofs and turrets both improbable and entirely inevitable.

Illustration, Del Coronado Hotel

The Del in those years still maintained the aura of the Gilded Age — turrets and verandas, deep shadowed corridors, polished floors that seemed to hold echoes of decades of footsteps. Palm fronds shifted in the coastal wind. White-uniformed staff operated invisibly. Somewhere, a band rehearsed, or a pianist tested a melody against the high ceilings.

The hotel was not just a resort. It was a meeting ground. Bankers, developers, movie stars, industry men from Los Angeles or the Midwest — even the Prince of Wales — they all passed through those wide doors.

Post-Depression Era

By 1935, Coronado had settled into a rhythm that felt precariously hopeful. The worst shocks of the Depression had passed, but prosperity had not fully been restored. On Orange Avenue, storefronts were open, their windows carefully arranged with confidence. A woman could step into Hartmann's Beauty Shop at 878 Orange Avenue and pay two dollars and fifty cents for a permanent wave, and a simple haircut cost fifty cents. Such transactions were quiet acts of faith in the town's future.

Automobiles now defined the street, unimaginable just twenty years earlier. At the Guarantee Garage at 931 Orange Avenue, shiny used sedans sat angled toward the sidewalk like promises waiting to be claimed. A nearly new V-8 Ford cabriolet could be purchased for under $500. A Standard Chevrolet coupe listed at $599. Even in lean times, mobility — literal and social — were still within reach for those willing to risk a purchase.

By the late Depression years and into the 1940s, Lawrence and Mabel had weathered the worst of the economic crisis and emerged with their financial security and social standing largely intact. The Great Depression had shaken confidence but also clarified who could endure. Those who remained — who continued to invest, build, and lead — found themselves included in a social elite defined less by old money than by continuity.

By the postwar boom, Coronado had outgrown its roots as simple vacationland. Growth and modernity pressed in from every direction. The continuity of people like Lawrence helped bridge eras. He represented the generation that had believed in Coronado early enough to stake both fortune and identity on it. From 1940 until his retirement, he was the Director of Coronado Federal Savings and Loan.

Over those decades, the pepper trees had grown taller, palms cast longer shadows, and board sidewalks were giving way to poured concrete. Neighbors came and went. But the bungalow on "C" Avenue held steady. Its terrace posts weathered. Its paint faded. By the 1960s, the house carried the layered memories of boarders, guests, children, and household conversations.

It had withstood wars that had been fought, children born, and were now adults with their own families.

At eight o'clock in the evening of August 29, 1965, Lawrence died at home. It was not in a hospital room or under the bright scrutiny of clinical lights, but on the screened-in back porch where he had spent countless hours listening to baseball games drifting through the radio — a slight, persistent echo of the boy he had once been. He was ninety-three. He had come west once as a man with nothing left to lose. His life, marked by tragedy, reinvention, public responsibility, and private endurance, came to its close in the familiar rhythms of the house he had helped shape.

Mabel entered widowhood with the composure of someone long accustomed to managing change. She filled her days with domestic routines and stayed active in the social circles that had sustained her for decades — charitable gatherings, visits with friends, the informal networks that defined her role in the community.

And the house with the porch facing "C" Avenue was still there one afternoon in 1970, when my father set a tape recorder on his knee.

Lawrence Safford Chamberlain, 1935

Mabel Powers Chamberlain

The House on "C" Avenue, Coronado, California

17

Inheritance

Their legacy isn't just in the life they lived. It's in the life you are still living, with pieces of them still guiding you every step of the way.

— Anonymous

Coronado, 1970

BY THE TIME ANYONE thought to ask Mabel about the past, much of it had already begun to disappear.

Memory did not vanish all at once. It faded unevenly, like a photograph left too long in sunlight. Details that once seemed vivid softened at the edges. Names detached from events. Stories shortened into anecdotes that could be repeated comfortably at family gatherings without reopening deeper questions.

She was an old woman when the conversations began. Her hands, once quick at the piano keys and restless in their creative pursuits, now moved more deliberately. The room where she sat displayed the accumulated presence of a long life — books stacked near chairs worn by use, framed photographs whose subjects belonged to eras younger listeners could barely imagine.

When my father asked about her grandfather, Billy Stealy, she paused. The orphan-train boy had always existed for her as a figure of someone else's telling rather than direct recollection. He had died before she could know him. Yet his story persisted in memory — he had been a child sent west among strangers. She finally spoke: "He was a drummer boy in the Civil War."

It was the kind of answer that satisfied practical curiosity while preserving the few details she knew. Other memories emerged more vividly. She spoke of music lessons and artistic pursuits, of social expectations that felt both constraining and motivating. She had spent years negotiating these differences, deciding which to embrace and which to release. Memory was as much a creative act as writing plays had once been.

❖

LAWRENCE AND MABEL'S DAUGHTER, Jane, grew up to marry a kind, soft-spoken man in 1939. But sometimes damage skips a generation, and the alcoholism and violence that plagued her grandfather, Ben McMeekin, reappeared in her temperament. Their union was dissolved and my dad, born in 1940, spent most of his childhood bouncing between grandparents and private schools, dodging the chaos unfolding at home. I never knew her, but my father has many memories of her taking him to the Coronado Playhouse in the 1950s, and she was one of the more 'stabilizing influences' of his childhood. I am grateful to her for that.

Mabel Chamberlain died in Oceanside in 1978, and with her passing, completed the long journey of migration from

Ireland to the California coast that had started in 1816 when an Irish couple boarded a steamship bound for America.

Epilogue

The address still exists.

121 Cedar Street in Manhattan appears on modern maps, reduced to a set of coordinates that can be reached with little more effort than entering a destination into a phone, which is exactly what I did on a hot July day in 2025.

But standing there in person reveals how profoundly time alters meaning. The tenement where Billy Stealy spent his childhood is gone. In its place rises a corporate office tower of glass and polished stone, its entrance framed by revolving doors and security desks designed for a world organized around efficiency rather than survival.

Pedestrians move quickly along the sidewalk. Most are focused on schedules, conversations, and digital screens. Few pause to consider what once occupied the ground beneath their feet. Cities reward forward momentum, their histories remain layered but invisible, accessible only to those who deliberately look for traces no longer visible.

I stood there longer than necessary, my teenage sons and husband indulging me for a few minutes more, yet anxious to keep moving. There were other things to see on our brief family vacation.

I tried to imagine the sounds that might have filled this space in the 1840s, which required an act of imagination that bordered on fiction. Tenement districts were dense with activity—the clatter of carts, the cries of street vendors, the overlapping languages of recently arrived immigrants negotiating unfamiliar terrain. Nothing in the present scene suggested that reality.

The building today offers no acknowledgment of its earlier inhabitants. Yet beneath the foundation lay the accumulated experiences of thousands whose movements helped shape its growth.

My third great-grandfather, William "Billy" Stealy, had been one of them. His removal to Randall's Island and eventual placement on an orphan train transformed his trajectory, but the urban world that shaped his early years remained part of his inheritance — and, by extension, mine. William Stealy exists now as both presence and absence. His name appears in military rolls, census entries, and marriage documents. They establish that he worked, fought, married, and died within the broader currents of nineteenth-century America. What they cannot fully reveal is how he experienced those transformations from within.

Standing at that intersection, I realized how temporary physical memory can be. Buildings vanish, neighborhood boundaries shift, and documentation and memories deteriorate. What survives is often intangible: stories preserved imperfectly, truths sent forward through generations who reinterpret them according to their own circumstances. Research offers partial recovery, but complete reconstruction remains impossible.

The experience did not feel like loss. Instead it suggested connection. The same forces that had compelled Patrick Stealy to leave Ireland, that had carried his son west across a developing nation, had also produced the metropolis now rising above their former lives. Movement creates absence even as it enables transformation. Understanding that paradox became central to understanding the family history

I was trying to write. Uncovering the past also requires a reckoning with the choices our ancestors made. It is tempting to assign the McMeekin legacy of slavery and pro-slavery politics to one branch of the family—label that line guilty and let the others remain clean. But history is rarely so neat. Responsibility, accommodation, and silence travel more widely than most want to admit. It lies in the ground beneath us as much as in the names we inherit—from the plots occupied by English settlers after Native dispossession, to the treaties and forced removals through which the United States drove Indigenous peoples from homelands held for millennia.

There is no simple repayment for inherited history. I cannot undo what they did, nor can I separate myself entirely from the benefits that flowed forward. What I can do is acknowledge the truth, refuse the comfort of selective memory, and make different choices in my own time.

Every ancestor carried hopes and fears, tenderness and cruelty, blind spots and convictions. Their decisions were shaped by the worlds they knew, some of them ordinary and some devastating in their consequences. We are shaped by what they handed down—but not bound to repeat it.

Billy Stealy, H.D. McMeekin, and Jacob Safford cannot tell us everything. But what we can learn from their stories — about endurance, movement, and the delicate construction of belonging — will continue to shape how their descendants and millions of Americans understand their place in the world.

I took one last look at the building before leaving. The past was not visible there. But it had not disappeared.

Addendum

Power Family

Mabel Lucile Power
Born: April 1, 1890 – Kansas City, Wyandotte County, Kansas
Died: February 23, 1978 – Oceanside, San Diego County, California
Spouse: Lawrence Safford McMeekin-Chamberlain

Mabel Lucile Power was born in Kansas City, Kansas. Her father, James Michael Power, was born in England in 1865 and immigrated to the United States, eventually settling in Kansas City around the turn of the twentieth century. Her mother, Margaret "Maggie" Gertrude Stealy, was born in Missouri in 1870. Together they raised their family in a region still closely tied to the legacy of frontier settlement and early urban development. Mabel grew up with siblings Margaret Gwendolyn, Walter William, and James Michael II.

By 1900, the Power family was living in Wyandotte County, part of the growing Kansas City metropolitan area, where economic opportunity and mobility defined daily life. Mabel came of age during a period of rapid change—when the frontier generation of her parents gave way to a more settled, urbanizing America. Her life would bridge those two worlds, carrying forward family connections rooted in early Kansas while moving toward the emerging West Coast.

She married Lawrence Safford McMeekin-Chamberlain, linking her life to a family deeply embedded in the early history of Kansas Territory. They lived in Coronado, California, where she spent her life. She died in Oceanside in 1978, having lived through nearly nine decades of transformation—from the post-frontier Midwest to modern Southern California.

James Michael Power
Born: March 26, 1865 – Newark, Nottinghamshire, England
Died: July 2, 1943 – Coronado, San Diego County, California
Occupation: Engineer (refrigeration)
Spouse: Margaret "Maggie" Gertrude Stealy

James Michael Power was born in Nottinghamshire, England, in 1865, part of a working-class family during a period of rapid industrial change. By his youth, England's manufacturing economy was expanding, but opportunity often required movement. Family accounts describe him leaving England at a young age, arriving in the United States as a stowaway on a banana boat, with little documentation surviving from his early travels.

He arrived in the United States via the Gulf Coast and eventually established himself in the developing interior. Over time, he built a career as an engineer specializing in early refrigeration systems—a field that was still in its infancy in the late nineteenth century. His profession required travel, installing and maintaining systems across different regions as the technology spread into commercial use.

By around 1900, he had settled in Kansas City, where he married Margaret Gertrude Stealy and raised a family, including their daughter Mabel Lucile Power. Later in life, he moved west to California, following the broader migration patterns of the period. He died in Coronado in 1943. Though parts of his early life remain unclear, his trajectory reflects a common pattern of the era: transatlantic migration, unstable beginnings, and eventual establishment through skilled labor in a rapidly modernizing America.

Stealy Family

Patrick Stealy
Born: c. 1816 – Ireland (likely Ulster)
Died: September 26, 1852 – New York City, New York
Occupation: Laborer / Clerk / working-class immigrant
Spouse: Mary Deegan

Patrick Stealy was born in Ireland around 1816, likely in Ulster, during a period marked by economic instability, sectarian tension, and limited opportunity for working families. By the late 1830s, like many Irish immigrants of his generation, he made the decision to leave. In December 1839, he arrived in New York City aboard the ship Rochester, traveling from Liverpool with his wife Mary and their young son Thomas. His migration placed him among the early wave of Irish families who arrived just before the mass influx of the Great Famine years.

By 1840, Patrick had established his family in lower Manhattan, living at 121 Cedar Street, near the waterfront and the commercial core of the city. This was a dense and rapidly growing immigrant district, where housing was crowded and work was unstable. Over the following years, the family grew, with additional children born in New York, including Thomas, Mary and William. Like many immigrants of limited means, Patrick's life would have been defined by manual labor, irregular employment, and the constant pressures of urban survival in a city undergoing rapid expansion.

He died in 1852 at approximately 36 years old, leaving behind a young family in a city that offered both opportunity and hardship in equal measure. His brief life reflects the experience of early Irish immigrants who arrived before the famine-era surge—men who laid the groundwork for the larger communities that would follow, often without leaving extensive records but whose impact continued through their descendants.

William H. "Billy" Stealy
Born: c. 1846 – New York City, New York
Died: before 1885 – likely Missouri or Illinois
Occupation: Civil War musician (drummer), barber
Spouse: Catherine "Kitty" Quinn

William H. "Billy" Stealy was born in New York City around 1846, the son of Irish immigrants Patrick Stealy and Mary Deegan. He spent his early childhood in lower Manhattan, in the dense immigrant districts of the 14th Ward. His mother died in 1851, followed by his father in 1852, leaving Billy an orphan at a young age. By about 1856, Billy had been sent west through the 'Orphan Train' movement and was living with the Mackey family in Illinois.

At the age of fourteen or fifiteen, on September 16, 1861, he enlisted as a musician in Company I, 50th Illinois

Volunteer Infantry. As a drummer boy, his role was not ceremonial but functional—relaying commands, maintaining cadence, and supporting the daily operations of the regiment during campaigns in the Western Theater. He served through some of the most difficult early years of the war including the battle of Shiloh, and was mustered out on September 27, 1864, after three years of service.

After the war, he settled in Missouri, where he married Catherine "Kate" Quinn in 1869. The couple had five children, including Margaret "Maggie" Stealy. Billy worked as a barber, a common and stable trade in growing Midwestern towns. He died relatively young, sometime before 1885, likely in his early forties. His life traces a clear arc common to many nineteenth-century Americans: immigrant beginnings in New York, displacement in childhood, military service in the Civil War, and eventual establishment in the expanding towns of the Midwest.

Safford Family

Jacob Safford ("Judge" Safford)
Born: August 17, 1827 – Royalton, Windsor County, Vermont
Died: July 3, 1885 – Topeka, Shawnee County, Kansas
Occupation: Lawyer, judge, civic leader
Spouse: Esther Mary Coon

Jacob Safford was born in Vermont in 1827 and came of age in a period when educated young men increasingly moved west in search of opportunity. Raised in a New England environment that emphasized education and civic responsibility, he trained in the law before joining the broader migration into the developing Midwest. By the 1850s, he had relocated west, part of the wave of professionals who followed settlement into new territories.

He established himself in Kansas during its formative territorial years, a period marked by rapid growth, political conflict, and institutional creation. Safford became a lawyer and soon emerged as a prominent figure in public life, serving as a judge and participating in the legal and civic framework of early Kansas. His career positioned him among the class of men responsible for shaping governance in a region transitioning from frontier territory to organized state.

Settling in Topeka, he kept active in both legal and civic affairs for the remainder of his life. He and his wife, Esther Mary Coon, raised a family during a period when the city was developing into a political and economic center of the state. He died of stomach cancer in 1885, at the age of only 58, leaving behind a record tied closely to the institutional foundations of Kansas in its earliest decades of statehood.

Jennie Marie Safford
Born: November 21, 1852 – Pontiac, Oakland County, Michigan
Died: December 10, 1921 – Oklahoma City, Oklahoma
Spouse: Benjamin F. McMeekin / P.C. Chamberlain

Jennie Marie Safford was born in Michigan in 1852, the daughter of Jacob Safford and Esther Mary Coon, at a time when her family was part of the westward movement shaping new communities beyond the established East. During her early childhood, the family continued moving west, eventually settling in Kansas Territory. By 1860, she was living in Topeka, where her father was establishing himself in law and public life during the turbulent territorial period. She graduated from Bethany College.

She grew up in a household closely tied to the civic and political development of early Kansas, experiencing firsthand the transition from frontier conditions to organized statehood. Her early years were marked by both opportunity and instability, as communities formed rapidly and institutions were still taking shape. This environment shaped a generation that bridged pioneer beginnings and more settled American life.

Jennie first married Benjamin F. McMeekin, linking two families deeply connected to the early history of Kansas and the broader westward expansion. She married P.C. Chamberlain who adopted her two children from her first marriage. The family added three more children and lived in Topeka. Her life reflects the broader pattern of nineteenth-century migration—born in the Midwest, raised on the frontier, and moved further west as new regions opened and developed.

McMeekin Family

Hayden D. "H.D." McMeekin
Born: January 3, 1822 – Nelson County, Kentucky
Died: September 10, 1885 – Wyandotte (Kansas City),
Kansas

Occupation: Merchant, Indian trader, hotel proprietor, lawman, territorial legislator

Spouse: Mary Jane Lawrence

Hayden D. McMeekin was an early frontier merchant and trader who moved west in the mid-1850s, settling first in Weston, Missouri, before establishing himself along the Kansas frontier. He operated a trading post near present-day Rossville and conducted licensed trade with the Potawatomi and later the Sac and Fox, placing him inside the structured but volatile system of government-regulated Indian commerce. By 1855 he had relocated to Leavenworth, where he became one of the early builders of the town, working as a merchant while also serving as deputy U.S. marshal during the turbulent border period and later as deputy sheriff of Leavenworth County.

H.D. played an active role in the early political and economic development of Kansas Territory. He was elected to the first territorial legislature, which met at the Shawnee Mission, and participated in foundational governance in the years leading up to "Bleeding Kansas." He also engaged in town development, including the founding of Indianola in 1854, a short-lived settlement along key transportation routes. His career reflected the fluid nature of frontier leadership—moving between commerce, law enforcement, and politics as opportunity and instability demanded.

By the late 1850s and 1860s, H.D. transitioned into the hotel business, becoming a prominent proprietor in Topeka. He operated the McMeekin House, a central gathering place for travelers, businessmen, and political figures. Contemporary accounts described him as one of the best-known men in the state and a widely respected figure among early settlers. In his later years, he moved to Wyandotte, where he died in 1885 at the home of his daughter.

Benjamin F. McMeekin
Born: October 1850 – Shelbyville, Hart County, Kentucky
Died: March 5, 1923 – Kansas
Occupation: Farmer / laborer
Spouse: Jennie Marie Safford

Benjamin F. McMeekin was born in Kentucky in 1850, the son of Hayden D. "H.D." McMeekin, an early trader, lawman, and territorial figure in Kansas. As a young child, he moved west with his family during the early years of Kansas Territory, growing up in a region defined by rapid settlement, political conflict, and economic upheaval. By 1860, he was living in Leavenworth, one of the earliest and most important towns in the territory, where his father was actively involved in business and public life.

Unlike his father's more prominent public role, Benjamin's life followed a less turbulent path shaped by stability rather than expansion. He came of age during and after the Civil War, remaining in Kansas as the territory transitioned into statehood. He later married Jennie Marie Safford, connecting two families deeply rooted in the early development of Kansas.

Benjamin spent the remainder of his life in Kansas, working inside the rhythms of local life rather than territorial politics. He died in 1923, having lived through the transformation of Kansas from a challenged frontier to a settled state. His life reflects the second generation of western settlers—those who inherited the instability of the frontier but built their lives in its aftermath.

Notes on Sources

This book combines documented family history with narrative reconstruction grounded in historical research. The lives of the Chamberlains, Stealys and Saffords are constructed primarily through surviving archival documents, including passenger arrival lists, United States census schedules, municipal death registers, and institutional records from mid-nineteenth-century. These documents provide key dates, locations, occupations, and household structures, but they rarely capture the texture of daily experience.

To help readers understand the world in which these families lived, the narrative draws on a wide range of secondary historical scholarship concerning Irish immigration, urban labor, public health crises, housing conditions, and religious and social tensions in key territories and states. Where direct evidence about the family is incomplete — as is often the case — the book reconstructs likely circumstances based on established patterns documented by historians and contemporaneous observers.

Descriptions of settings such as Ward 14, retail employment practices, tenement life, and responses to disease outbreaks are therefore informed by period reports, municipal investigations, activist literature, and modern historical studies. Narrative scenes are intended to remain faithful to the historical facts while conveying the emotional and social realities of immigrant life during this period.

Spelling variations in historical records have been preserved where relevant, and ages and dates reflect the inconsistencies typical of nineteenth-century documentation. The aim of this work is not to claim certainty where history is silent, but to recover — as responsibly as possible — the lived experience of individuals whose stories were only briefly archived in official ledgers.

About the Author

Parker Corbett is a writer and independent publisher focused on narrative American history. Her work centers on the intersection of personal story and national transformation—how ordinary lives are shaped by war, migration, economic upheaval, and the long reach of historical forces.

With a background in communications and public opinion analysis, she has spent more than two decades studying how stories are constructed, remembered, and often misunderstood.

Carried West began as a search into her own family's past and became something larger: a broader examination of westward expansion, the Civil War generation, and the making of modern America.

A Note from the Author

If this book gave you a new perspective on migration and American expansion, I would greatly value your review. Reviews matter as signals to other readers that these stories are worth encountering. Even a brief, honest review helps keep books like this visible.

This title is part of a larger body of work published by Unbound Press, dedicated to overlooked histories, marginalized voices, and rigorously researched nonfiction. If this approach resonates with you, I invite you to explore the full catalog. Each book asks a similar question: whose stories were carried forward, and whose were left behind? More titles like this are available at www.UnboundPressBooks.com.

Thank you for reading—and for helping these histories continue to be read.

More Books by <u>Unbound Press</u> are available at
www.unboundpressbooks.com

Frontier Chronicles: Stories of the Contested American Frontier

Ghost Dance War
The Last Uprising of Native Nations

Women on the Prairie
Stories of Grit, Survival, and Unbroken Spirit

Spirits Unbroken: Indigenous America Series

Echoes from the Eastern Shore
Twelve Native American Chiefs and the Fight for the
Atlantic Homelands

Last Council Fires (coming soon)

Twelve Chiefs of the Colonial Southeast

Fault Lines: Titanic Micro-histories

Steerage and Steel
The True Story of Titanic's Crew and Immigrants

Ladies First
Titanic's Reckoning with Wealth and Worth

American Silencer

A History of Political Violence in America

America Uncovered

<u>Dawn of an Empire</u>
St. Augustine and The Spanish Founding of America

Women Between the Lines: Overlooked Lives That Shaped History

<u>Mothers, Sisters, Soldiers, Spies</u>
Women at War in American History

<u>Troublesome Women</u>
America's Whistleblowers, Cultural Pioneers, and the Women Who Changed the Rules

---

<u>Hitler's Jewish Wife</u>
The DNA of Eva Braun & The Secret of The Third Reich

www.ingramcontent.com/pod-product-compliance
Lightning Source LLC
Chambersburg PA
CBHW020912060726
47591CB00004B/1202